COMING OUT GOLD

A Quest for Sexual Purity

ROB JOY

malcolm down

PUBLISHING

First published 2018 by Malcolm Down Publishing Ltd.
www.malcolmdown.co.uk

British Library Cataloguing in Publication Data
A catalogue record for this book is available from the British Library.

ISBN 978-1-910786-42-0

Cover design by Esther Kotecha
Art direction by Sarah Grace

Printed in the UK by Bell & Bain Ltd, Glasgow

Endorsements

This book is a voice for those in a wilderness. The issues which are addressed in this book are those that the church is afraid to talk about. It is written with honesty, integrity and transparency. I would highly recommend this book.

Daniel Chand
Evangelist

Brutally and refreshingly honest, Rob's story is sure to be a healing balm to many, many lives. A story of sin, shame, hurt, pain and of seeking, restoration, love and mercy. Utter sexual confusion and moral anarchy is sweeping the world right now, both in the public setting and in the private recesses of many lifestyles. This book will surely help the powerful grace of God to infiltrate these areas of guilt-ridden brokenness, bringing the freedom and wholeness so desperately needed!

Jarrod Cooper
Senior leader, Revive Church

Coming Out Gold is not just a book about sex and pornography. It is a book about the destructive nature of sin but also the incredible grace of God and the redemption that is found in Jesus Christ. I admire Rob and Lydia for their honesty and courage and I am encouraged that no matter what our struggle is, there truly is hope and freedom found in Jesus. Rob has found and is continuing to find that freedom, and I believe that many others will also be helped as he shares his journey in this book.

Andrew Murray
Generation Builders ministries

Rob Joy is like the prophet John the Baptist, a voice crying in the wilderness. His book, *Coming Out Gold* hits major issues, but then give some valuable answers and keys to freedom. He deals with the shame and guilt, then love and forgiveness. It is so refreshing and transforming. Rob doesn't condemn but offers hope and freedom to people, especially in world we live in today. You can see from this book Jesus truly is the answer!

Dr Mark R. Van Gundy
President of Kingdom Legacy Network, a part of Churches n Communites International.
Senior pastor of Church of Destiny, Tottenham, London
Missionary and part of World Outreach Ministries, Marietta, GA, USA

There are a number of things that are endearing about the author of this book but the one that draws you to Rob Joy more than most is his willingness to be utterly transparent and vulnerable when telling his story.

To Rob, sex addiction is serious business because it has the ability if unchecked to destroy your very soul. It is for this reason, with no holds barred, he draws the battle line and encourages the reader to engage in a holy war until it is utterly destroyed.

Rob has been there, done that and wears the badge, he knows what works, where the pitfalls are, but more importantly how to cross the finishing line and declare victory. He is quite simply extremely qualified to guide those who today are bound and chained in their prison of sex addiction and lead them to the place of total release, which he has realised through much trial, can only be found when exposed to the love and power of God.

I am certain that this book is going to be a powerful tool that will bring great freedom to many people, and consequently it needs to be put in the hands of all who need to be set FREE!

Ken Gott

International director of Transform Our World and founder of House of Prayer Europe

Coming Out Gold sheds bright light on a dark subject that has tormented many. It will give hope to anyone who is bound in sexual addiction and help others understand the pain and shame of this prolific problem. Rob Joy writes with raw honesty and heartfelt compassion. He has unique insight and wisdom, and is qualified from the vantage point of having walked this out in his own life. This book removes the cloak over a secret problem and points to a way out.

Jo Naughton

Founder, Healed for Life and pastor, Harvest Church, London

The unrelenting spiral of guilt and shame resulting from a lifestyle of sex addiction and pornography is a subject rarely addressed from the pulpit. Many sufferers are confronted by pride, ignorance and a lack of compassion from people hardened and insensitive to these issues that hold so many captive. Rob Joy addresses this pandemic head-on in an authentic, discerning and grace-filled book.

I've known Rob for many years. His heart and yearning to see souls set free and living in the fullness of Christ is truly inspirational. He is a passionate disciple whose honest, open and quite often forthright approach stirs up the desire to follow Jesus wholeheartedly.

In his book, *Coming Out Gold* Rob goes beyond an exercise in understanding what the Bible says; it is a weapon against one of Satan's biggest tools in keeping God's people from being free and effective. While Rob focuses on his personal testimony around sex addiction, the pages are filled with kingdom perspective on how to confront and win the spiritual battle against habitual sin that is keeping so many locked into a shame-filled, unrelenting, bitter cycle of hopelessness. It is a passionate insight into living a life of freedom in Christ Jesus, being transformed by the Holy Spirit in the joy of His presence, and the importance of protecting our intimate connection with the Father.

Matt Hall
Pastor, Trinity Life Church, Royston

Coming Out Gold is a much-needed alarm bell to wake the Church to face and deal with the on-slaught of a sexualised society and the effect that it is having in the Church and the nation to-day. Writing from the freedom that he has personally experienced from sex addiction, Rob speaks into this challenging area with compassion, grace and wisdom, but also with a deep conviction that things can change.

Through biblical teaching and practical steps, Rob shows how the power of sexual addiction and the shame that comes with it can be dealt with in people's lives so they know they are forgiven, can live in freedom and are empowered to live as an overcomer.

I wholeheartedly recommend every parent, church leader, youth and children's leader read this book to not only see the reality of what is happening but to be equipped to face it head-on and deal with it graciously, in our children, church members and ultimately our nation.

Clive Urquhart
Senior pastor, Kingdom Faith church, Horsham

Brutally honest, real, gritty and transformational. I've no doubt at all that many will find hope, healing and peace through reading this book by Rob, a man who is living proof that only Jesus Christ can transform our lives – and he does!

Carl Beech
President CVM, Lead Pastor, Redeemer King

Acknowledgements

With my sincerest appreciation I want to thank several people for making this book a reality.

Jo Naughton, the advice you gave me not only massively improved this book but also me as an author. I was stunned by the simplicity of what you said and how it had such a huge impact. Paul Naughton, thank you for being on the end of the phone, in a coffee shop somewhere whenever I need to chat, and for cheering me on.

Jarrod Cooper, Andrew Murray, Daniel Chand, Matt Hall, Carl Beech, Mark Van Gundy… thank you for taking the time to read and endorse this book and for being inspirational men of God. I honour you all.

Michael Odendaal for the initial front cover design and to Malcolm Down and his amazing team who took that design and with a few tweaks turned it into what it is now.

Ken Gott, my spiritual father, thank you so much for always thinking the best of me even when I really wasn't being the best version of myself. A father sees beyond behaviour and beyond failure and brings a timely word to build a son back up. I will never forget the way God used you to speak such life back into my broken heart.

Thank you to all who contributed to this book, whether editing, layout, proof reading, graphic design and all the hours that went into turning a manuscript written by an uneducated man into a resource we can all be proud of. Malcolm Down especially, thank you.

Thank you to those buying it and reading it. I pray it touches your heart.

To my family who allow me time to pray and think, dream and write. Lydia Joy, my utterly inspirational wife and very best friend. You never quit, you never spoke negatively about me or to me, you are a seamless source of hope and encouragement to me and I admire you and adore you to all the worlds and back again. Thank you, gorgeous. Callum, Emmanuel, Apphia, Samara and, of course Kiarna, my precious kids who make up the Joy Family.

Jesus, the very biggest heartfelt thank You is Yours. You put all these people in my life, You gave them the wisdom and the compassion to walk with me and see me as You do. Jesus, You alone deserve the highest praise and the ultimate honour. I am always stunned by You. xXx

Contents

Foreword

If I were to speak with eloquence in earths many languages, and in the heavenly tongues of angels, yet I didn't express myself in love, my words would be reduced to the hollow sound of nothing more than a clanging cymbal. (1 Corinthians 13:1)

Love is large and incredibly patient. Love is gentle and consistently kind to all. It refuses to be jealous when blessing comes to someone else. Love does not brag about one's achievements nor inflate its own importance. Love does not traffic in shame and disrespect, nor selfishly seek its own honor. Love is not easily irritated or quick to take offense. Love joyfully celebrates honesty and finds no delight in what is wrong. Love is a safe place of shelter, for it never stops believing the best for others. Love never takes failure as defeat, for it never gives up.
Love never stops loving. (1 Corinthians 13:4-8)

Growing up, I went to many weddings and heard these verses quoted in the ceremony, and if I'm honest, I was bored of hearing them in that setting. I thought it was a cop-out. 'Just read any verse about love to fill the gaps.' Which was why at my wedding I remember specifically not having them read. I was bored of people preaching about love and especially, as a woman, getting love preached at every women's conference I went to. Never did I think these would be the verses that got me through some of the toughest situations I had faced, and now have such a deep meaning to me and I would have them read at my wedding if we did it over again!

I felt I should write a little chapter for this book when Rob told me what he was writing about. I felt that the partners of those who have struggled with these addictions, or any addictions, needed to hear my side too, not just to encourage but to know they are not alone. There is hope and there is a future for you, so don't give up.

I read somewhere recently that one of the reasons so many marriages fail nowadays is because we have this mentality of 'If it's broken, get a new one' whereas in generations before, if something broke, you fixed it. It may have taken more time and more effort to fix it, but that is just what you did. Going out and buying a new one wasn't an option. We live in a society where if your relationship isn't working quite as well as it should, or its broken in some way, rather than spending time on mending what's broken, we go and get a divorce and find a new, 'better' version. This was never an option in my mind. I am lucky enough to come from a great Christian family, with loving parents, who worked through things together and never gave up on each other. My grandparents, although not Christian, were still together and I remember celebrating their fiftieth wedding anniversary, and they were still as much in love as they were when they met. I loved it. I never experienced divorce or a broken relationship up close – thank You, Jesus.

I was nineteen when I met Rob and in my last term at university. My dad had come to get me to bring me home for the Easter holidays. We were sitting in Wetherspoons and he said to me, 'Do you fancy helping out with this outreach event we're doing for the estate kids? There's some guy coming to share his testimony.' Immediately I thought, 'That guy is my husband.' I brushed it aside as I thought I was just 'being a girl'! I didn't know how old he was, what he looked like. All I knew was he was 'some guy'.

When I got home I saw a book lying on the kitchen counter and asked about who it was. It was written by the guy who was coming to share his testimony at this outreach. I thought I should read it just to find out if what I'd thought was God or me – for all I knew, this guy could be married with kids! And if I'm honest the picture at the front wasn't the most flattering. I read it within two hours and afterwards was a little more convinced that this could well be my husband. But I wasn't about to go shouting it to everyone.

Little did I know my mum had had a dream a few weeks before of me in a veil about to get married, so she had it in her head that it wouldn't be long before there would be a wedding.

On the day of the event I didn't think too much about it, really; I just got on with helping Dad with the worship and setting up, my mum was in the kitchen as she was doing the lunch for all the kids, and the organiser (an amazing woman, Margaret Macormack) was chatting away as usual and dropping hints about this guy to me. (She was trying to set us up!) I was standing with my brother, Joe, who was sixteen at the time when Rob walked into the room. Joe turned to me and said very bluntly, 'You wish!', which always makes me giggle. Rob walked past my mum and she had a vision of a plane flying past with a banner that read 'Lydia's husband'. No one had said anything to anyone at this point, God was preparing us for what was to come.

Rob and I went on our first date a couple of days later and basically got engaged there and then. I bought my wedding dress a week later. I had heard God, Mum had heard God. Rob had thrown 'a fleece' (see Judges 6) out to God on that first date to test to see if I was the right one. We had gone to an arcade and we were at one of the grab-a-toy things where you never win anything. He said to God, 'If I grab two in one go, she's the one!' And yes, he grabbed two in one go! I don't think anyone else needed any more convincing. We talked about getting married in the August which was only a few months away.

During the next few weeks and months it was pretty tough. Rob had just been launched into his ministry and his pastors at the time didn't think it was right for him to be dating, so we were told not to speak to each other for a while. I got on the train to go back to Weston-super-Mare where I was studying from Sunderland where Rob was living. I was in tears, not really knowing or understanding what had just happened. I had heard God, Mum had heard God, Rob felt he had heard God, yet we were not together, not able to talk or even think about marriage.

It didn't take long before we couldn't help but speak to each other. Then in the June Rob had a 'picture' (a vision) from the Lord to confirm that we were to be together and that we were to get married, but he was to wait. This was because I had applied and been accepted to go to America for nine months to study worship, starting in the September. So while I was there, only able to speak to him via Skype every two weeks, he and my mum planned the whole wedding!

I returned in the June of 2010 a totally different person; I had encountered God so deeply out there and it was so clearly God's plan for us to have that extra time to sort stuff out personally before coming together and getting married.

Obviously I was aware of Rob's past. I had read his book, I had heard him share his testimony, but I think I was slightly naïve to think that there wouldn't still be stuff to work through. I wasn't fully aware of the nature of his addiction at the start. I was aware of the struggles. But I think because of the environment I had grown up in, I was unaware of how his upbringing may have affected the way his brain worked from being exposed to porn at such a young age and everything else that he went through.

As the wife of someone who has come from a background like Rob's, you have to be aware that it may not be an easy ride. I was still young. We were married a few days after I turned twenty-one and we were thrown into this crazy time of living by faith for our day-to-day needs, travelling the country while Rob preached and I would do some worship or ministry, having such a passion for revival and really feeling that something was about to break out in our area. It was a great season! But suddenly it was over; we moved to another town to plant a church, we had our first child together all within the same month. Rob was busy preparing for the launch of the church and I was busy, struggling with being a new mum in a new town, away from my family. This is when stuff really began to show up.

I would come downstairs and find Rob weeping and see a smashed-up phone on the floor. At the time I was more annoyed that he had broken the phone as to why he had, but I could see there was something that was really breaking Rob's heart. He would tell me snippets and I would try to help, but I wasn't equipped to do so. I knew he would tell some of the guys at the church to pray for him and there were seasons where they would and then it would stop. It was difficult to see my husband fighting so hard to do the right thing and get help. He had a couple of sessions of therapy but was told to stop, so he did.

I remember a time where we were away ministering and something happened which meant that this issue was now more public knowledge. The guy who we had planted the church with had a vision where Rob had crows' claws stuck in him and he was fighting to get these claws out. It was hard for me to face, as now I was more publicly the wife of someone who struggled in this area and I didn't want people to feel sorry for me. I wanted people to stand with us and walk us through. But no one seemed to want to. Due to the immediate fallout and obvious and understandable hurt, I believe people on both sides were not able to see clearly.

We carried on as we were building the church which was growing fast and we were having more pressure added to our already weakened shoulders. In this season we were too busy, building church and being in positions which our giftings didn't suit. And this meant we were running on empty. We were seeking God to find the next sermon, not to be in His presence.

I was struggling with being a new mum and being a pastor's wife and being the worship leader and helping run the internship, and also trying to help my husband in this battle he was fighting largely alone. I felt guilty for not praying enough for him, I felt guilty for not feeling like I was enough – which is a lie, but one that the devil uses to fuel the fire of this issue. I knew Rob loved me. I knew God had called us to be together, and we just plodded through.

It wasn't until we had just had our second child that everything fell apart. It all came out. Rob had been watching a lot of pornography and often acting out those desires with other women via text (sexting). And it came out in such a way that we were not prepared for. We lost everything in the space of a morning. It was a horrible, horrible feeling. I still see the faces of those who were meant to be our friends pouring shame and guilt onto Rob, out of their own hurt.

Yes, I was hurt. Yes, my head was full of everything that had just happened. But as they were telling Rob he could no longer be in the church but that I could, I felt an incredible desire to stand with Rob, to be the one that wouldn't leave him in the gutter as if he was worth nothing. I don't know if God has given me a gift of forgiveness, but as they were looking at me to see if I was going to leave him, I knew that was not an option. God hadn't left him. God still loved him. God still had a future for him. And I had also seen Rob weeping and crying and fighting to beat this thing behind the scenes. Yes, there were things Rob could have done, but shame is a massive thing that holds people back from doing the right thing. Rob is a fighter and I knew I was to be in his corner at this time, telling him to get back up again. Rob at the time was at rock bottom and we had two young kids to think of too. So we went to my parents' house, and there began the restoration of our marriage and our ministry.

It was at this time God began to speak to me about those verses in 1 Corinthians 13. Love 'keeps no record of wrongs' (verse 5, NIV). 'Love never stops loving' (verse 8); 'Love does not traffic in shame' (verse 5). Even through my hurt, my questions, the one thing that was stronger than all of that was the fact I was not about to give up on Rob, and my desire to not be seen as the poor wife or the stupid wife still standing by her husband. I could imagine what people were thinking. But I chose to ignore it and listen instead to what God was saying, what the people around us were saying who were willing to walk us through everything. The devil was not going to win.

I am not an aggressive person by any means, but when something gets under my skin, I want to fight. I remember growing up fighting with my brother; this indignation would take hold and I just wanted to fight till I won. I was going to fight for our marriage until we won. There were times where I would feel anger towards Rob, out of the hurt that I felt and the mis-trust that was now there, but I wasn't going to let it rule. Just as Jesus was betrayed by us, just as Jesus was hurt by us and our mistakes and our adultery, He still loved, He still forgave. If only the Church would get this.

'As far as the east is from the west' so our sins are removed from us (Psalm 103:12, NIV). Romans 2:4 tells us God's kindness leads to repentance. So many verses are flooding my brain. How could I not forgive, how could I not walk with Rob through this? How could I not be there to let God fix us?

It wasn't easy. I lost friends, I lost my church. I lost my nice house – we felt we had to move from the town to really seek God and have immediate family support. But would I change a thing now? Looking back, obviously I'd rather it hadn't happened, but what we have learned from it, I would not change. Our eyes have been opened again to the schemes of the enemy to wipe us out, our eyes have been opened and our hearts reopened to the desire for revival. My understanding of God's forgiveness and love for us has gone so much deeper. My relationship with God has gone so much deeper. My relationship with my husband is so much deeper. He is not living under shame any more. He gave me beauty for ashes, gladness for mourning and praise for despair (see Isaiah 61:3). God's goodness is all around, even through the pain and the heartache.

I hope my side of the story has helped. I'm not perfect, I have struggled along this journey but I know that we are called to be like Christ. If I am called to be like Christ, then I am to love even when I feel betrayed, to forgive those who hurt me. To fight for the things God has given me. I am not a victim. I am a fighter for the ways of God. Forgiveness is worth fighting for. Your marriage is worth fighting for. Your future is worth fighting for. You are worth fighting for; just as the woman caught in adultery was worth fighting for and she was spared from death by Jesus because no one could cast the first stone (see John 8:1-11). Be the champion of the ones who are wanting freedom and desire freedom whatever the cost.

From before Rob and I met, God had a plan and a purpose for us. He spoke to us every step of the way. He knew what we would face. He knows what you are facing. He knows what you are feeling. Let Him comfort, let Him heal. Let's be fixers of the broken. Let's be Jesus to this broken world. Let's be love.

Lydia Joy, autumn 2018

Introduction

Right now I am sat in a half-decent hotel in London. A basement room with no windows. I am carefully, prayerfully and fearfully beginning to write the introduction to this book you now hold in your hands.

I fully appreciate that you may have little or no faith in Jesus, and you may never have been in a church or even formed an idea as to what or who you believe in. This book is not written to address a church issue, or a secular issue, but it is specifically written to address what I believe is a global epidemic. I wholeheartedly believe this is a heart issue and therefore impacts everyone in society.

The Church has its own ideas. The politicians and educationalists and law-makers have their opinions, and the medically gifted and psychologists and the like have their facts and figures to throw into the mix. All valid and all valuable. I am simply sharing my testimony, my own thoughts and convictions and being another voice that speaks into this monster issue. It is a confusing, messy, ugly, painful, exciting, arousing, tormenting topic. At least, that's my experience.

I am writing this book as a Christian with very strong and passionate views taken from the Bible which I unashamedly believe in as the way, the truth and the life of Jesus (see John 14:6). I am certainly not wanting to offend any other views, but I am definitely wanting to challenge some of them. I will use language that to some outside of the Church may seem strange, like 'I heard God' or 'I had a vision' but I would simply encourage you to read this book with an open mind and weigh up the content as a whole, not just from a few sentences or the odd chapter.

If you are a non-Christian or an atheist, then you may actually be pleasantly surprised at a lot of what I say in this book. I do make much apology for where I believe the Church has largely failed to rightly address sexual addiction (or all addictive behaviour, for that matter) and represent what I firmly believe is a very loving, gracious, forgiving, long-suffering and yet still holy God.

I believe I have heard from God to write this book, but it is a burden to me. It is with great trepidation that I write because of the nature of it and the transparency of it, and the rawness with which it must be written.

I have fasted and prayed, studied and sought counsel from my closest friends and those I am accountable to, and I have wrestled to the point of tears as to know exactly what God would have me share and teach within these pages. By His grace I hope to empower you as a reader to set either yourself free, or a loved one, or just simply join the holiness movement that the Lord desires to raise up and send out into the darkest of places. I am fearful as I write, but I know I am qualified to do so considering the topic and my 'history'.

My passion in part is to show those of you who do not believe in Jesus that God (when rightly presented by others) is far more loving, kind, interested and available than you may be aware of – He is not distant and angry; He is for you, not against you – however, without watering down the very real need for people like you and me to humble ourselves and repent and learn to trust in Him.

My name is Robert Joy, I am now thirty-nine years old. I have been a Christian since 2005. Since that glorious day when I accepted Jesus and asked Him to forgive me I have never once doubted the reality of the Lord's existence. I was completely addicted to drugs, alcohol, sex and pornography and in my old lifestyle I even gave myself to forms of witchcraft and the occult.

I was a man hell-bent on destruction and was never once half-hearted in my pursuits. I found after approximately one year of becoming a Christian that not only my addiction but also temptation to take drugs were broken entirely. I have been clean of drugs ever since. However, I would be lying if I said that all my addictions stopped at the same time. Porn, masturbation, and sexting has seemed to plague my life and walk with God for well over a decade. It has nearly destroyed everything, not least my own soul.

Writing this book is extremely emotional for me because I am having to face head-on the giant that has taunted me and mocked for so long. The giant that has held me back and nearly ruined my reputation, family and friendships. I still grieve over the ones I did lose and threw away. It also nearly destroyed my destiny in God. I am having to face a ruthless, evil enemy that longs for destruction in our lives so he may gloat and boast and feed off our misery.

Coming Out Gold is not just about porn and sex addiction, it is about you, wherever you have been, however you have fallen. It is about you realising the eternal and significant value you have in God. It is also a message to churches and leaders across the world to better equip themselves with mercy and grace and encouragement and restoration for the endless stream of hurting souls that have become bound by this epidemic.

It is a lifeline to the drowning, a warning to the proud, and an encouragement to the champions that are fighting back all across the globe right now with a sense of the Holy Spirit's indignation. I want to awaken your zeal to rise above the degrading stain of this particular sin and disease. It is a clarion call to us all that although there is endless grace in Christ, there is also still today a very serious call to live holy and passionate lives.

For the reader that doesn't believe as I do concerning the awesomeness of Jesus, then I just hope and pray that during the reading of this book you at least consider that Jesus may actually love you, care for you and want you after all. Which I assure you is the truth.

The facts and figures on this issue are excruciatingly painful to read and hear. The river of the modern-day Church, media, celebrities and everyday people is littered with dead bodies. Men and women that have fallen into gross sin and lost sight of their real identity.

You will hear me saying often 'I saw' because I hear frequently from God in that way. I enjoy a relationship with the Lord that is very revelatory and I find this exciting when it is anchored to a deep knowledge of the Bible and intimate prayer life. By saying 'I saw' I simply mean I had a vision or dream.

I saw a river that was flowing at some speed but it was being dredged. As the water level lowered I began to see body parts (limbs) that had been amputated and cast away. I felt the Lord showing me this because on His heart are the countless souls, ministers, ministries, celebrities, husbands, wives, fathers, mothers, sons and daughters that have been amputated from the body. The Bible refers to the Church as the body of the Lord (see Ephesians 5:23; Colossians 1:24). People have been cast away in disgrace when God never intended for them to be forgotten or rejected.

I had a vision as I woke up this morning of a horse that was wild and free. This horse was standing close to a huge concrete wall but there was a vast open space all around. I then heard the Lord say 'Cornelius' and turned to Acts 10 to re-read that story. Cornelius and his household were considered unclean by the Jewish people due to their being outsiders.

Peter the apostle received his own vision as he sat on the roof, praying. In the vision God opened his eyes to see incredible grace and a new wave of salvation that was about to crash over the non-Jewish people as a sign that God forgives everyone and has no favourites. Peter, as a Jew, believed certain foods were unclean but God showed him that if He called something or someone clean then clean it was. The Holy Spirit was poured out over Cornelius and his entire family and so began the outpouring to a non-Jewish people. Suddenly revival started in a place and with a people that had previously been labelled as unclean, unworthy and out of favour.

Prophecy from 30 May 2018

I am seeing something about to change in the nations of this world and it really excites me. I believe that countless thousands of out of favor and written off people are going to experience an incredible grace and outpouring of the Spirit of God. It will be in such a way that those who had previously spoken against them will be stunned to see the restoration of the Lord in their lives. I believe the Lord is going to correct many leaders who have discarded broken and hurting people because of ignorance about their weakness. A beautiful repentance and forgiveness will rule the day. Many that have said, 'I cannot fellowship with that person or that group' will realise the Lord Himself is calling them clean and they can rise up and eat (fellowship) with them again. I believe it will be a precious mark of grace and unity. I believe the Lord is saying, 'Those who others have called unclean and unworthy will begin to see their own needs and their own shortcomings.

'There will be a new apostolic grace as we enter an age of restoration never known before. This age will represent the soon coming of the King and the Holy Spirit's urgency to reap a mighty harvest.

Forgiveness will be poured out like a river bursting through the dam of shame, and judgement as those who have been self-righteous are brought to their knees as I reveal to them their own sins and their own weaknesses. I will show this broken world that all have fallen short of the glory of the Lord and I will stun this world as I forgive and heal sins that man refuses to forgive. I will show mercy on whom I will show mercy.

'The result will be that the horse and its rider will bolt from the wall of shame and judgement and will once again enjoy the beauty of the open space in Me.'

I believe we must not call unclean what God has called clean. We must see others how He sees them if we want them to walk as He does. Of course there must be repentance and faith in Christ, but grace paves the way to a new day of clean.

God wants people healed, restored and joined together again so they may function effectively once more. In my experience the Church is often far too trigger-happy when it comes to shooting down the wounded soldiers or the immature 'have-a-goers'; those who for whatever reason choose not to confess their struggle or sin. On that note, and with a mixed feeling of grief over those I hurt, and the friendships I lost because of my sin I will now confess to you some of my journey. Not so I can glorify the devil or justify myself (I am already clean because of the word He has spoken – John 15:3) but to liberate what really is a massive army of hurting people and shame-filled sons and daughters that He calls by name.

I am not going to name any names. I am certainly not going to shame others who were involved in either the sin itself or the handling of it. The manifestation of my sin (which was pornography and sexting, which was starting to lead towards deeper desire/need/compulsion to act out) may be different to yours, but I believe this book will help to reveal, heal and deliver you. I thank God for the leaders out there He has used to help restore and whom have clarity and awareness of this issue, but often it can be abusive and damaging.

I pray now for the others who may not see clearly on all of this within our communities to hear from God and respond in love, and offer themselves as vessels and instruments of profound healing to the Lord's precious people. I did not just flirt with a little porn here and the odd immoral conversation there, I was utterly bound and drowning in sexual sin. It was never illegal but was definitely highly immoral.

As a leader, a pastor, an itinerant preacher, a husband and a father, I risked everything for a quick fix, which could have been viewing pornography, or as it developed and became a more aggressive oppression in my life, a text conversation with any woman I could find in that moment. The risks became more dangerous, the people became more personal and the conviction (although it was always present) lessened as the years progressed. I shared at times with my wife and with certain friends around me, but the fear of losing my reputation and ministry stopped me from fully revealing the depths of my struggle.

I was drowning and I was destroying so much good that God had built through me and the team around me. We were winning souls (seeing lives transformed) and we were attacking the enemy's kingdom. Partly due to a massive lack of understanding concerning the spirit realm and the ways of our enemy, the devil, I was walking daily into his plan to discredit and destroy.

Satan is ruthless in his pursuit. Once he has a person or a ministry in his sights he does not let go until he has utterly destroyed them, or been cast down with the authority God has fully given to His people. I did not have any kind of ongoing affair or love relationship with anyone but I was obsessed with sexually explicit conversations and inappropriate text messages with other women. I never stopped loving my wife and the idea of losing her and not being with her would always bring me to tears, yet something that was beyond reason alone was driving me on in my hunger for sexual encounters.

I personally believe along with many others that sex addiction is very real. The victims of it are endless. I hurt a lot of people when my sin was exposed and for that I am deeply sorry.

I always was, yet still I continued. Sin brings consequences despite the Lord's full forgiveness. I sometimes have dreams that the people I hurt forgive me and there is a reconciliation of sorts, but you cannot unscramble an egg. You have to live with the consequences. I pray for those I hurt and I hope they thrive under the healing and grace of an Almighty healer and redeemer in Jesus Christ. I am not for one second playing down my sin or the hurt that it caused when I say what I am about to say next, but those suffering from sex addiction are often also victims. Our fight is 'not against flesh and blood' (Ephesians 6:12, NIV) and we preach this in our churches, but do we actually believe it and live it and wage spiritual warfare like we understand it?

I would be delighted if through the writing of this book the eyes of those outside of our Church community would be enlightened to see that the world issues are not just political but they are indeed spiritual, and there is a realm outside of the one we see naturally that dominates and drives what we do see.

You are not my enemy and I am not yours! Satan is the enemy of our soul and he delights in using us against each other so we destroy one another.

The name of Jesus is brought into disrepute and the world around us is constantly being shamed. Ignoring the devil and playing down his involvement in these issues does not stop him, it only empowers him. I know (as I was told repeatedly) that the devil cannot be behind every lamp post waiting to attack everyone, but he is certainly real and certainly at work and has a vast army at his disposal. He wants to afflict God's beloved people. Whether you know Him or not, you are loved by God.

It was only when I started to break free of some very poor teaching that I was able to better equip myself in the battle. I will offer in these pages some weapons of spiritual warfare I believe will be a great resource to fight this epidemic as well as all other battles we face.

If only our politicians could admit their need for God. If only the Scriptures were held up in parliament and in our schools and our justice systems. I am convinced we would see incredible change.

You may be merely treading water right now as the waves of sin crash around you. You may even be under the water holding out for your last breath before the seas of Satan's schemes envelop you and wipe you out completely. You may have given up all hope and lost sight of Jesus altogether, if you knew Him. Like me you may have experienced a great deal of shame or been rejected, but this book and the beautiful work of the Holy Spirit and some practical and spiritual nuggets I hope to offer you here will give you wind in your sails and faith to go on. I was holding out for the 'wham bam thank You Jesus' miracle encounter, but it was a very long time in coming. I rejoice that it has for some others I know of, but for me it has been much more about the process than the destination. I am not confident that I would have the grace and compassion I have now for those stuck in sin cycles and despair if I had not experienced such a ruthless, decade-long battle with lust.

God never ever wanted me to be hurt, or those I led to be hurt; He is never like that. But He does promise to turn everything that the enemy uses against those who love Him for good (see Romans 8:28). Let this book do just that. As my friend Paul Naughton recently said to me concerning the writing of this book: 'Tell the truth and shame the devil. He is the one who has held you in bondage of guilt and sin consciousness so smash him to bits with this book. It is his shame, not yours.'

I have had bishops in Africa that lead hundreds of churches come to me weeping after I have spoken on this subject, confessing their sin and battle. That is glorious, isn't it? Is that not what we should believe for and experience? A revival of grace and healing and faith for the journey ahead? Not just in our churches but in the media, businesses, families, streets?

I have had some incredible prophecies given to me in quick-fire succession over recent months from anointed men and women of God that have been used to remove shame from my life and empower me back to the harvest field and platform ministry. I will share some of these prophecies with you because God is no respecter of persons (see Romans 2:11, KJV) and I believe these words of life may also set you free. I will also share some of my own stirring thoughts with you as to just how grave this situation is and why it must be addressed, confronted, and overcome. Please join me in the following pages with as honest a heart as you can muster, and with an openness and willingness to admit it is a worldwide epidemic, and it is an unacceptable evil in our generation that only the work of the Holy Spirit and the willingness and surrender of man can conquer together.

I know this issue hugely impacts others, and often innocents are left scared, confused, angry, alone. I want to offer my sincere sympathy and love to those who were faithful and through their spouses or loved one's infidelity or addiction were wounded and/or mistreated.

My wife, Lydia, was one of those people and asked me if she could write the foreword to this book offering her side of the story in the hope that it might also help others.

Chapter 1: Sexual Confusion

As I finished this book I had a very detailed and powerful dream that I knew God wanted me to add here to really set the scene for this book and to give you incredible hope.

In the dream I was seeing someone going through an internal and external battle with sexual confusion. A man who had been for an operation to become a woman and was now alone in a bedroom looking into a mirror and feeling utter confusion and fear as both male and female genitalia could be seen (God clearly isn't shocked or freaked out or unwilling to discuss these issues) and the realisation set in that this decision was now permanent. In the dream this person was so broken, confused, ashamed and angry. I watched as the dream unfolded and this person stormed into the office of the surgeon and screamed in anger: 'Why didn't you tell me it was permanent? Why didn't you give me more facts? Why didn't you notice I was confused?'

In the dream this person was traumatised by the thought of being trapped like this forever and was very desperate. I woke up.

I am fully aware that this is such an incredibly sensitive topic and I do not feel in anyway qualified or equipped to speak much into this personally other than by sharing the dream itself.

God is not afraid to take on the big topics and put them on the agenda of His people and the world, so neither should we be. There have been times, though, when the Church has been very insensitive and often ignorant, and for that we must apologise.

So many precious people have been hurt and offended and we have since lost our voice as the Church to speak into these matters. Surely, if we really have the heart of God then we must pioneer the way for a sexual revolution.

I believe the dream was from God and so I stand secure on that. I believe God wants to be involved with those who admit they feel confused sexually, but I also believe in His respect of free will. He will not force anyone to stop doing what they believe is right. I passionately hold to the 'one man and one woman in the covenant of marriage' attitude that I believe the Church should absolutely be lifting up and holding as heaven's values and the way of the Lord.

The Holy Spirit began to birth in me a real indignation and zeal to speak into the global crisis that is sexual confusion. It is not just about porn, or masturbation, or lust, or adultery, it is about confusion. It is about a generation that have not been giving the true facts and God the Father's heart on this issue. It is about people believing they are something or someone they are not and despite what the media wants to portray as 'normal', it is not normal that so many people, young people, are so confused and beaten up in their minds by popular opinion and social media. In being encouraged to explore different expressions of their sexuality, there is a 'go with the flow' attitude that is literally capturing the souls of God's people and leaving them internally broken and filled with fears, regrets, confusion and shame.

I have just finished filming for the BBC on the topic of porn addiction. I was part of a very varied panel including a female porn film producer and a gay porn star who believes porn is therapeutic and encourages others to try it. With opinions that suggest porn should be used in an educational way to teach children how to use condoms, we need to face up to a code red security breach on our souls and our children's futures.

I believe we absolutely cannot stay silent any more. We also cannot be self-righteous and religious about it and cut ourselves off further from being a credible voice to the world around us. We as the Church should have the answers because we know the truth in Jesus. Those reading this outside of the Church community have the right to know what we believe and why, and also to consider our views and decide for themselves if they agree or not. We cannot approach this merely from a scientific viewpoint, or medical research alone; this is a spiritual battle and one that can only be won by addressing the fight in the arena of the spirit.

Our governments and educationalists and our psychologists cannot be left to make these decisions alone. With all due respect, we as the Church do not get to make them either, we declare them according to what God has already spoken so clearly in His written Word with a heart of love, and we pioneer a new and living way in the wisdom, knowledge, grace, forgiveness and beauty of our King. We remove sexual confusion, we hold up the Word of God and we stop burying our heads in the sand. We speak about this from the platform, in kids' church and youth ministry, on the media, social media, because we are the ones who are supposed to be walking intimately and in relationship with the author of sex; the creator of sexual desire and appetites and expression.

We are the ones who must stop hating and judging and assuming we are the spiritual police when we are supposed to be the spiritual doctors and nurses, not religious legalists who name and shame and cast aside the broken and sexually confused from our own church communities.

If we believe that how the Church acts affects the nation, then we must look at the absurd thinking, demonic attacks, sexual confusion and 'anything goes' culture and repent for letting this happen. Then we must study, pray, talk, love, forgive, heal, believe and come to a unity on this. Then I believe the commanded blessing of God (see Psalm 133) will fall like a mighty wind upon our leaders, churches, communities and the nations of the world.

If a nation or a city experiences a natural disaster such as a flood and many homes are swept up by the violence of the waters that have escaped the safety of the banks, then rightly so, we as humans rush to help. The first thing on our minds and the priority of our mission is to get as many as we can to safety, to rescue those whose lives are in danger. We do whatever we can to stop further destruction and of course mourn and grieve with those who have lost their treasures and their family members. We invest financially in the rebuilding project and we take up offerings and collections to try to relieve the pressure from those most affected and to be a blessing to them. That is simply human nature and good will in action. The Bible says: 'However you wish to be treated by others is how you should treat everyone else' (Luke 6:31).

Shouldn't we be rushing to the aid of the sexually confused who, for whatever reason, find themselves overcome by the flood of sexualised opportunities that their soul has been saturated with for decades?

Shouldn't we stop pointing at the 'sinner' and start pointing to the Healer? The Redeemer? I sinned, I made many stupid mistakes, I failed others as a leader, as a family man, as a friend, I got it wrong, really wrong, but whatever the reasons and whatever the history, finding myself in the flood of sexual confusion and addiction is not the end of my story and it is not the end of yours. There is grace, forgiveness, healing, power and victory. A glorious inheritance is waiting for you.

I am not belittling sin, I am not excusing sin and I am not suggesting the Church should not bring about some discipline when appropriate. But, I am saying, we need to mature in this area of crisis; we need to mature in love, grace and forgiveness. We need to mature in knowledge and in the prophetic and spiritual realm if we are going to clean up this mess. Then we can rescue the hurting, heal the broken, and of course mend the banks so the flood becomes a flow. Then the rivers of life take God's holy course rather than us accepting a sexual holocaust.

Here are a few facts surrounding porn and sex addiction you may not be aware of:

Porn use increases the infidelity rate by 300 per cent

40 per cent of sex addicts lose their spouses, 58 per cent suffer considerable financial loss and about a third lose their jobs.

In America 47 per cent of families admitted porn is a problem in their home

68 per cent of divorce cases involved one partner meeting someone else online

2.5 billion emails sent or received each day contain porn

Every second over $3 million is spent on porn on the internet alone

Search engines get 116,000 queries everyday related to child porn

35 per cent of all internet downloads are porn-related

One-third of porn uses are women

Teenagers using porn have lower levels of sexual self-esteem

Teens using porn become massively vulnerable to sexual development

Every thirty-nine minutes a new porn video is uploaded to the internet

These really are just a small few of the facts I could share.[1]

No wonder we are so sexually confused and filled with shame!

This is an epidemic, this is a spiritual attack, this needs addressing. This must be done now. Let's go!

If you want to pray this prayer with me I believe it will help you focus and draw the most from this book:

> God, if I am sexually confused, if I have fallen into a trap, if I am off course when it comes to your precious plan for me, my sexuality and my life in general, then I give You permission to change my heart and mind. Remove the lies and dethrone sexual confusion. In Jesus' name.

Remember this book is not only for addicts, it is for anyone.

If you want to take this even further and so as to avoid the strong temptation to speed-read through this book and risk missing what God wants to do through it, I encourage you to pause now, put some music on by someone like Eric Gilmour (my personal favourite) which you can find on YouTube and give some time and space to let the Holy Spirit speak to your heart and bring some healing to your soul.

---

1. Source: https://www.charismanews.com/us/73208-15-statistics-about-the-church-and-pornography-that-will-blow-your-mind (accessed 18.10.18).

Chapter 2: The Iron Curtain of Shame and Division

Although the origin is debatable, and may be attributable to Joseph Goebbels, many attribute the phrase 'the Iron Curtain' to a speech given by Winston Churchill regarding the communism that had descended after the Second World War. It was a political, military and ideological barrier that the Soviet Union erected to try to keep out any contact with the West and non-communist nations. Stalin was at the helm, physically speaking, but behind all of this was an unseen enemy called Satan. This unseen enemy loves to bring division and war and hatred into our lives.

I am not a historian, I am merely pointing out a few facts regarding the 'Iron Curtain' because during prayer this morning in preparation to continue writing this book it was a vision the Lord gave me concerning the subject we are dealing with here. I believe Satan has used the world to raise up an iron curtain of division within the Church and our communities so as to heap shame and isolation on people. Although not limited to porn and sex addiction in his efforts, I believe it most certainly is one of his greatest tactics to continue to bring strife, conflict and division among us. Leaders are isolated in this battle. Church members are isolated in this battle. Families are isolated in this battle. The devil is rubbing his filthy hands together as he sits back and watches how so many of us will not talk about, address or confront this iron curtain of addiction.

Shame and hopelessness that this sin has brought into the Church runs rife and spills out onto our platforms and into the hearts and minds of men and women all across the world. The iron curtain must come down, and the only way it will is through truth, love and the power of God.

I wonder how many people will read this book and will honestly say that this subject has not or is not in some way affecting them personally? Marriages are being battered by this issue. Children devastated by it. Ministries are weakened or ruined, and the witness to the world so often compromised by a well-meaning saint who ends up crossing that line.

Politicians, celebrities and everyday people are ravaged by this crisis, and the Church often sits in silence and pretends it is not also affected by this the enemy of our soul. Enough is enough!

Before we can go any further and I want to share something I believe God has given to me over a decade of dealing with this issue. We must face up to the truth together that *sex addiction is real.* I am not just talking about a few people giving in now and then to the temptation of pornography, or a couple of fallen leaders being exposed in adultery; I am talking about a global pandemic of exponential proportions.

I urge you to open your eyes and see, if you have not realised yet, just how violent an attack this is against God's holy people and the nations of the world; a spiritual army that plans the destruction of men led by a merciless, evil enemy. We can't just hope this will go away.

Arm yourself and get involved in the battle for our churches' inheritance and birthright, which is holiness and purity. Arm yourself so our families, towns and cities can be flooded with love and truth and many set free.

God is looking to raise up some 'enforcers' of His Word and His cross in this generation so that the iron curtain and the bondage of confusion, sexual abuse, broken relationships, mistrust and discredit can be stopped.

If you are honestly not affected and you never watch porn, never flirt, never cross that line, and you can offer that testimony to the world, then I salute you and I cheer you on with the utmost sincerity. However, please do not use your freedom from this sin to attack; we are all susceptible to different sins! Be like the Lord and fight valiantly for the freedom and victory of His people in love, wisdom and compassion.

Woven throughout the spiritual iron curtain, the Lord showed me rods of iron that reinforced this demonic attack against the Lord's people. Rods of shame and condemnation, guilt and despair. We must remove these things from the heart of the Church and the mind of the people because they only ever empower the enemy and weaken our understanding of the power of the gospel.

I sincerely believe the Lord's Church, His people, form God's intended core of every community. I believe the Church is made up of broken, hurting people like you and I coming into right relationship with a holy God through the sacrifice of Jesus Christ. The Church should be the heartbeat of every society; it should love others, release the presence and power of the gospel and bring spiritual change and therefore physical change.

As I was just writing all this, my flow was interrupted by a phone call from my sister. It was about her as a mother, seeking my advice concerning her eleven-year-old son who is being deeply upset by his new football team, due to the barrage of swearing and grossly sexualised conversations these other kids are having – making up sexualised incest stories and talking about porn, and all manner of other comments being made. These kids are eleven and twelve years old and they are already well and truly corrupted by this epidemic, this plague; this iron curtain that seeks to isolate them and keep them away from ever knowing their true value and identity and the purpose and love of God in their lives. My sister's cry was, 'What do I do as a mother in this situation?' and the cry of this book is, 'What do we do as a Church in this situation? What do we do as a nation?'

It is everywhere. It is in our schools, in our homes, in our workplaces, on our TVs, on the internet, and it is in our churches and it is in our leadership teams and it is a very, very big deal.

I am being asked by more and more leaders to speak about this and I would urge church leaders not to just make this issue a men's breakfast event, or a seminar during the main conference at the church for those who may feel they should attend. Let's get this on the main agenda of the church, raise the awareness levels and offer the grace, love and empowerment of the Holy Spirit to speak into our hearts and minds. Only by being really vulnerable and real can we ever break free and enter into the fuller meaning of Christ's life for us.

I believe a strategic heavenly plan is being revealed to us so as to focus our joint efforts on overcoming this battle. Winning is what Jesus does. He always wins, but He does so through our full cooperation and partnership with Him. We are co-labourers and it is a mucky business, so let's become unshakable and unshockable as we face this together.

As I was praying and waiting on the Lord earlier, I felt I heard God say, 'I am going to give you heaven's strategy and clarity' and I believe He was referring to this book, and future ministry into this area. I am excited about this. After more than a decade of fighting, losing, winning temporarily, losing some more, fasting, praying, crying and being 'dealt with', I can see the light at the end of the tunnel.

If you are like me, then your journey in this battle may seem like a game of tennis. You watch as your walk with God (or marriage, or relationship) goes backwards and forwards and you feel like the ball being smashed around the court. You fly forwards just to find you are now flying backwards and then forwards again, and then backwards. Or maybe you have just giving up entirely? You are hiding and refusing to actually fight any more? You are tired and confused and despondent and you have had enough?

Let me introduce you to two of my real-life friends that love God, have encountered Him and been filled with the Holy Spirit, yet still have very real ongoing battles with lust and porn etc. Men (although it is a female issue too) who I know well and have walked with closely at times. I can vouch for the sincerity of their hunger to live holy lives. Everyday men who have approached me and shared stuff with me and that I now honour as the courageous ones. I do not judge them and I do not reject them. I do not think less of their passion for God and revival and service. I just love them, pray for them and with them and I know I can also share my deep wounds and struggles with too if need be.

These real testimonies will speak to you in a personal way because for many of you there will be a powerful similarity in what they feel and how they face this issue, and what you are dealing with yourself. In sharing these stories we are not glorifying the devil, we are disarming him. We are saying, 'Stop, enough is enough' which is what the word 'rebuke' means. So, let's rebuke the devil together and stop this onslaught of demonic attack against the bride of Christ, the Church, change the atmosphere of the Church towards those who deal with this issue, and put an end to the devastating effects it has on our souls and our society.

I have changed names to protect identity.

A courageous two

Gary

I am sixty-five, been married twice and I have been a committed Christian since the age of twenty. As a child, I was sexualised around the age of five by my father who was into pornography. At boarding school, I suffered sexual and physical abuse from the headmaster. I was converted to Christ in 1972 out of a background of casual sex, taking psychedelic drugs and seeking truth through occultism and Eastern religions.

Because of my background, I have always been vulnerable to the temptation of pornography, even when the only means of gratification were soft porn magazines and blue movies at cinemas. Mostly, I managed to resist the temptation. Being married helped in this.

Unfortunately, my wife went through a time of mental and physical ill health in her early sixties and the medication she received suppressed her desire for sex. Since 2004, we have been unable to have any kind of sexual relationship. This has coincided with the increasing easy availability of hard core porn on the internet. This has led to many difficulties and battles over recent years. I would successfully resist temptation for long periods and then stumble in sin. Then it would be a regular problem for a while until I got rid of my laptop. Problem solved until I had access to another computer. Basically, it was a sin cycle and addiction that I could never fully break.

I had got to know Rob and over time I felt to open up to him about my struggle as I knew he had been though similar problems. Knowing that he had been through the same struggle because he was so honest about it gave me the courage to open up to him, knowing I wouldn't be judged. He recommended a website called Covenant Eyes[2] which scrutinises what a person looks at on the internet and will advise a trusted friend or friends if something of a pornographic nature is being looked at it. This accountability has helped enormously. As I have constantly prayed for the addiction to be broken and maintained accountability, the Lord has helped me greatly and the desire for pornography has been largely replaced a by real desire for purity. I am still on my guard and know that I can never afford to become complacent. However, I am really praising the Lord for the victory over porn addiction He has brought me into.

Yes, the Lord is calling all of us to a holy life and to abstain from all sexual immorality (see 1 Thessalonians 4:3). The Church has mostly learned not to beat up its members that still wrestle with nicotine addiction, so let's not beat anyone up that may have a very real sex addiction, or as in my case, has been diagnosed by a therapist as having a 'love addiction' that drives men and women to seek out gratification and affirmation and 'pain relief' during stress and emotional woundedness. The devil has been oppressing God's people for a very long time now and he is good at what he

2. https://www.covenanteyes.com (accessed 17.7.18).

does. But let's remember he can be overcome by 'the blood of the Lamb' (what Jesus did for us on the cross, breaking the power of sin and separation from God) and 'the word of [our] testimony' – and that we triumph 'because [we do] not love and cling to [our] own lives' (Revelation 12:11).

Before we continue, I want to share a prophecy I was given by a worship leader when I was preaching in the Philippines a few years ago: 'I see you in a prison and you are shackled and I see you suddenly stamping your foot and the shackles breaking and as they break I can see countless people behind you and their shackles are broken too.'

This prophetic voice did not have any idea about my addiction to porn and sexting and the person was quite courageous to share this publicly with the guest preacher, but I knew what God was saying and it still resonates in my spirit years later. By sharing my story in this book and encouraging some of my friends to do the same, we are stamping our feet in holy indignation and coming out of our chains; we are inviting a generation to join us and be set free in Jesus' name and walk in victory and fruitfulness. Will you be one of those whose chains are broken? Will you allow the Lord to deliver you and then use you to deliver others? I pray you will and I pray the Holy Spirit right now arrests your heart and mind and gives you incredible zeal to be free.

David

When Rob asked me to write my testimony for the book, initially I was hesitant as I knew if I was going to do this it would require me to be fully transparent in my story in order to reach others battling with similar issues.

I first met Rob and his wife in 2012. I am so thankful for him; there has never been any judgement or criticism but just a desire to help and walk with me. I thank God for this.

Here's my story.

My parents had become Christians in 1987. I was raised in a Christian home from the age of six. I had found pornographic magazines in my house, which had belonged to my father, and they aroused a curiosity in me about sex.

As a child I recall being touched sexually by a close family member. This caused me to question my sexuality (yet I have never been attracted to the same sex) at around eight years old, so I engaged in homosexual acts with a friend who was the same age.

I knew deep down this was very wrong and I knew this was against what I believed, but again, it was more out of curiosity… and although I hated this, there was also part of me that enjoyed it although I knew how wrong it was.

I knew from a young age I loved Jesus and I was baptised around ten years old. I was even told I'd have to leave my school if I didn't stop telling people about Jesus and how He loved them and wanted to save us from hell. I also remember vivid reoccurring nightmares of the devil in a physical form grabbing me by my hair and saying horrible stuff and that I belonged to him.

During my teens I began to notice girls taking an interest in me and I also was very attracted to them and developed a few casual relationships. I believe this was deeply rooted in a feeling of wanting to be valued and accepted.

At fifteen or sixteen I started to smoke weed and experiment with different drugs and alcohol, which only fuelled my desire for women and sexual relationships. I had various girlfriends and a number of 'one-night stands'.

I also became involved in crime. I was dealing some drugs for a local dealer and I got further into drugs and alcohol, which quickly escalated and eventually ended with being sentenced to two years in a young offenders' prison for a robbery and a stabbing.

I was tired of my life and I was tired of who I was and what I was doing. I hated myself, I wanted to change in my heart but didn't know how; I had always given myself over so easily to my desires. I wanted a fresh start.

On my release from prison in 2002 I had made a decision to return to my childhood faith and try to live right. Yet, on the day of my release a few mates wanted to throw a little party, and some of the girls there were paying me a lot of attention. A few drinks and a few hours later, I had slept with my mate's cousin. She said she loved me and missed me while I was away and she made me feel like I was worth something and I was accepted.

About five months later I decided to enrol in my church's Bible college for a year and was a resident there, which gave me the opportunity for a clean break from the old circle of friends. After the first few months I started a very trusting relationship with a girl there. We came very close one night to sex; this was a massive distraction during my time at the college and I left in 2003 after the year was up. I think even then, deep down there was no real repentance, although I wanted to do what was right.

A few years later I started smoking cannabis again. Then I met another girl that I married in 2005 and we had a son together, but the relationship ended in divorce. The relationship was wrong from the start and I knew it deep down, but I just wanted to fill a gap in my life and have a family. I confessed to her that I had had a number of sexual relationships during the marriage. I really hated what I'd become.

This led me to a long period of broken relationships, sex, drugs and alcohol.

I knew what a mess I had made of my life but I couldn't see a way back. I struggled with bouts of depression, suicidal thoughts, hatred of myself and what I had done.

In 2009 I met another girl who I had a relationship with – she made me feel so good, she would always compliment me, she made me feel so valued and I really loved being with her. She eventually broke it off in January 2010 and I was devastated. I began to deal with it in the only way I knew how, by getting high and drunk. This went on for a number of weeks and I felt an overwhelming sense of guilt and condemnation. It was unbearable, I really didn't want to live any more.

Alone in my flat for a few months I wrestled with what I was. I felt very low. One night I had drunk a lot and I had fallen asleep, but I woke at 3:23 a.m. and I just felt something say to my heart: 'Read Luke 9:23.'

I grabbed my dusty Bible and found the passage. It's where Jesus says: 'Whoever wants to be my disciple must deny themselves and take up their cross daily and follow me' (NIV). I knew God was speaking to me!

I called my old pastor the next day and told him what had happened. He spoke and prayed with me and led me through a prayer of repentance. I decided to start living for Jesus. We began a weekly men's meeting in my flat and I became involved in the church.

I met my now wife of almost seven years and we have two children together. I'm active in the church leading our youth group with my wife, daily following Jesus and declaring His truth over my life. I'm far from perfect but His grace is enough and His love reaches further than any sin! I have to remind myself that I can't be defined by my weaknesses; because of what Jesus has done we can start over again.

Even a few years after I came to repentance and even after my second marriage, I learned I was still subject to temptation and became emotionally involved with another woman at work. It went from the odd 'hello' to texting to a kiss to very nearly becoming full sexual intercourse. I knew this was not right and broke things off. I struggled with heavy guilt and shame not only for that but for my past.

I lived under a cloud of depression for so many years but I've always known that God has had His hand on me. I had been getting news of friends that were dead – killing themselves and dying from other things, and they were not even as bad as I had been!

I believe if we repent, God will save us and set us free, but we can still choose to be enslaved again, we can get out of the lifeboat – I know that my heart's desire is to walk right, I want to pursue holiness, I want to pursue my wife's heart and please God. But we can choose to walk in freedom or walk in our own desires; we can choose our lives or we can deny ourselves, take up our cross and follow Him.

These men are real people. They are my friends in churches across the UK and I know they are lovers of God and passionate about holiness. Their battle is real. Their enemy is real. The addiction is real. But I am not excusing bad behaviour, far from it; my message is all about deliverance and freedom.

Jesus loves the Church! I want us as the Church to become a more effective witness. The men who have given their testimonies have done so to give you hope, and for that I believe we should salute them. The man or woman who feels no conviction, is unwilling to walk with accountability in this or does not have a deep-seated desire to stop whatever form of immorality or addiction has taken hold of them is in a very desperate place. That person must potentially face isolation from the local church and body of believers but *wherever there is a glimmer of repentance or the smallest sign of a desire to change, then we must respond and do so with knowledge, wisdom, grace and faith for the victory and future of that person.*

Of course, like with all addictions, it is imperative that the addict first recognise they have a serious issue and also that they cannot cure themselves.

Pray this with me now:

God, I am tired of feeling ashamed, broken and confused. I give You permission to speak to me about shame and more importantly, Your righteousness and how You see me. I give You permission to come and love the broken me and the hurting me and impart Your living, breathing love to my weary soul. In Jesus' name.

Again, I would strongly encourage you to pause now and reflect and soak in worship and allow your heart to draw towards His. This book has absolutely no power in it to change you unless the Lord is in it.

Chapter 3: The Collapse of the Iron Curtain

The iron curtain is mostly surrounding the mind. For that reason we must go after the thinking most sex addicts and those bound by porn will experience about themselves and about how God views them. We must also overcome the fear of man and the opinions of men. This is a crippling, debilitating weapon forged in hell itself and we must win that battle early if our troops are to be all they were created to be. The fear of man really is a deadly snare (see Proverbs 29:25), so let's address this together. Let's start by looking at what God thinks and declares over you and let's at least set the record straight on how heaven sees you. Then we can build from there and form new thoughts and new passions together and realise how awesome we are in Christ.[3]

I am utterly convinced that although we are talking about the sex addiction issue, these very timely truths will greatly benefit every kind of addict and ex-addict. The reason I am not a fan of 12

---

3 My YouTube channel, Kingdom Cause Community, has many fifteen-minute videos speaking more on this subject that you can use alongside this book.

Step programmes is because they do not really teach someone that they can be *ex*-addicts and a 'new creation' (2 Corinthians 5:17). Get this book into the hands of every addict you know and those coming from that world, as it will definitely empower them.

Shame is a master player in the grand scheme of Satan to bring the Lord's people into a weakened state. Because sex addiction brings a great measure of shame (I will talk about holy conviction in a moment, which is a beautiful thing), all those within the Church community that have this issue going on in their lives will find it usually results in a secret affair with this sin. I have found that people in the Church find it a lot easier to confess anger issues, or trust issues, or smoking cigarettes than watching pornography. Or using one of the many hundreds of apps and internet opportunities to talk sexually with someone online. Sin is sin, but, there is such a profound connection with sexual immorality and shame because the enemy of our souls knows only too well that sexual sin is the only sin that is against our own bodies (see 1 Corinthians 6:18)

Shame always follows an 'episode' and shame always empowers the next. Shame says, 'Look at you, you are dirty!' whereas holy conviction says, 'Look at you, you are far too valuable to be behaving like this!' and if the Church could get to grips with this and start leading from this place we would see more people set free.

I have sat in many rooms with leaders and spiritual fathers who have heard my confession or caught me out and have (with good intention, I am sure) done nothing but shame me. I have left those meetings feeling worthless, not convicted, ashamed, not challenged, beaten up, not bettered, and ridiculed, not released. I do not believe this was their intention, but we must mature. We must ensure the person in our care comes away believing that failure is not final.

A while back as I was praying in my office, I had a vision of a huge billboard outside my shop in Luton. It was an advert for the L'Oréal company who have the slogan 'Because You're Worth It' and it's always a stunning woman or two waving their beautiful hair around, covered in loads of professionally applied make-up and saying (usually in a sultry, sexy voice), 'Because I'm worth it.'

 In this vision this huge billboard was on full display. Laying in a comatose state underneath the billboard due to alcohol, drugs and homelessness, was a man who most would not give the time of day to. He was completely broken and addicted, filled with shame and hopelessness. He was lying half-dead underneath this advert filled with models, make-up and fancy products (perhaps a bit like many modern-day churches?) and the advert said: Because he is worth it.'

The Holy Spirit showed me in a moment that although this man had completely lost his way, he had not lost his worth. The way to set that sinner free is not to tell him how sinful he is, but rather how valuable he is to a holy God. We did not deserve the cross and we never will.

Jesus died upon it because every addict, every porn star, every sinful saint, every leader entrapped in sexual addiction was, and still is, worth it! You are precious, you are beautiful, you are unique, you are special. The iron curtain of shame and division is lying to us all, this spirit of despair and judgement is confusing the life out of the Church.

In my opinion, too many leaders are either judging those who have fallen, or they are ensnared themselves and too afraid to come out for fear of shame, isolation, rejection and a loss of reputation. Well, it is time to come out, and come out we must, as gold (see 1 Peter 1:7); refined and purified by the fire of God's holy love that does not consume but brings clarity, purity and incredible value to our souls.

Every time you or I make that poor choice to view pornography, it is ultimately because we have never realised our true value. Would the golden bar that has been refined so intensely that its value is exponentially increased ever choose to return to its dross? Would it rather not fight to stand in its new position? Yes, we were filled with dross of every kind, and so much so there was no hope we could ever stand before a holy God, yet while we were still sinners 'Christ proved God's passionate love for us by dying in our place while we were still lost and ungodly!' (Romans 5:8).

He saw us as we were before humanity fell away from God and before Satan gripped our prideful hearts. I do not view the filthy images on the internet primarily because I am sexually aroused (of course, that is involved) but more so because in that moment I am believing a lie. I am clearly believing that I am impure or else I would not dare to look upon something that is impure. If I realised my true value and purity and position in Christ, would

I not rather say a firm 'No!'? Would I not turn and flee from it, knowing that it could corrupt my thinking and my emotions and my body?

It is learning, as my dear friend and mentor Mike Parkyn always drives home to me so passionately, that living out of our new creation, our new 'spirit man', that we overcome the flesh and evil desires that are often so prevalent within us.

The wall of shame collapses when we realise just how precious we are to God and how He sees us in the light of our many imperfections.[4]

What is shame?

What is shame? Why does it cause such division and isolation within the Church and the world we live in?

Shame is to the soul what cancer is to the body. A ruthless evil that eats away, destroying a person and leaving them weak and vulnerable and defeated. Until, of course, that shame comes under the blood of Jesus and the full healing which is readily available through faith.

Shame is basically a feeling of being dishonoured, worthless,

---

4 I have a series on my YouTube channel titled 'You are so lovely' which is taken from the Song of Songs, several fifteen-minute videos teaching and praying through this very special book written, it is believed, by King Solomon. I strongly advise you to watch and re-watch them until something inside you turns towards the truth of how He sees you.

inferior, disgraced. I guess the trump card of shame would be to feel devalued. Of course, we can bring that feeling upon ourselves through poor decisions and loose living, and also others can heap shame upon us in their response to our actions and choices.

Jesus comes to restore value to us all. Shame comes to displace it, or cause a soul to lose sight of the value it has to the Father. Shame is a treacherous heavy weight that bears down on your own soul and conscience, leaving you apathetic, unable to pray as you ought, insecure and often defeated. It is a life killer, a destiny killer, it is a serial killer!

However, like all serial killers it can be caught out through a specific pattern of behaviour.

Shame is an illegal criminal act against the cross and the soul that has been saved by it. God permits and imparts conviction of sin, but He does not permit shame and He never will this side of Jesus' death and resurrection. Now, I must clarify that Jesus will use the shame you feel to bring you to your senses so you cry out to Him for forgiveness, but once you accept Jesus as your Saviour, then shame is destroyed fully, freely and forever.

Shame makes you feel dirty, unclean and guilty. Shame has a way of making you feel dirty even when you have not sinned. Shame is basically you not forgiving you. That sin still feels unpaid for even though Jesus has fully paid for it at Calvary. Shame is a weapon of mass destruction to the body of Christ and to the whole world. We need some courageous people to remove the stigma and shame of porn, sexual immorality and all addictive behaviours.

Will you be one such person?

Will you rise up in such a way that others are released to at least begin their journey of freedom? In a safe place surrounded by non-judgmental friends and leaders who are willing to pioneer the road to sexual healing and deliverance within the body of Christ? This is the generation to do just that.

I believe it must start in the Church and then affect the whole world. You and me, everyday people that want so badly to give everything to Christ and the call of God upon our lives, but seem to be held back by this invisible force that constantly trips us up.

Well, I can see shame, I can see it for what it is, and I am here among others to call it out, call it what it is and displace it. Remove its lying, cheating, damning power from those whom God loves and delights in regardless of their sin, crimes against Him and His body.

I am convinced that if we remove shame we would see a harvest of saints delivered and empowered and released back into community; I believe we would even see global impact for the Lord. Some may disagree with me, but I am persuaded that harsh rebuke when their sin is exposed is not only unhealthy and unfruitful but actually partners with Satan in ruining that soul. This model strengthens the rods of shame rather than tearing that wall down.

Shame creates an invisible wall of division. It separates souls from their healing. It isolates ministers and ministries and breaks relationships, marriages and friendships. Yes, it is a serial killer.

Maybe you can now recognise the pattern in your own life?

To catch a serial killer the police usually have to find their pattern. Are you in the shame division? In your mind? In your view of yourself? Are you lost in repeat defeat and a vicious sin cycle? Are you reading this book because it is potentially the last chance for your soul to be set free and set on fire? I pray that you feel a quickening of your soul right now and your faith is lit. I pray for hope to arise as shame begins to recognise it is eviction time, and in the name of Jesus Christ I rebuke your shame and declare over you the goodness of God. I declare over you the blood of Jesus to remind you that you are already clean if Jesus is your Lord and Saviour.

Wherever shame is, sin will be close by. Shame will derail your destiny quicker than anything else, in my opinion. It is so often a master of disguise too, so we cannot be without the Holy Spirit and His ability to reveal even the most hidden and ingrained shame. Revelation and relationship flows out of the very nature of the Holy Spirit. Before we go any further with teaching, testimony and prophesy we must make sure you are filled with God and know how to really engage your spirit man. Then you can enjoy intimacy with God the Father that only the Holy Spirit can bring. The spirit man is simply the new you. The you that has been restored back to an intimate relationship with God. The spirit man is grown as a new baby is, through the right food, care, development, but of course the food is spiritual, the care is born out of your times with the Lord and with other Christians.

Pray this prayer with me:

God, I thank You that Your loving kindness is better than life itself and You never once intended for me to live under a cloud of shame. I choose today to receive Your forgiveness and healing and ask You to continue that work of grace in my life. In Jesus' name. Baptise me now in the Holy Spirit.

Chapter 4: Repentance and Correction

A very misunderstood and poorly taught verse in Scripture is 1 Corinthians 5 and the whole 'expel him from the church' thing. There is absolutely a place for this to be enforced in certain situations. and I myself would do so if it warranted it. I do not believe in 'cheap grace'[5] and turning a blind eye to ongoing sin in the Church, especially when it has such a corrupting effect on other believers and the effective witness of that family.

The point I am urging you to look at closely here is whether that person has any sign of remorse, desire for change and the working of repentance in their lives. Are they broken by their sin? Are they desperate to be free? Is there a bigger picture to look at? Are they sincerely seeking God and serving Him passionately in many other ways yet there is this 'thing' that seems to grip their heart and mind and continues to cause failure in one or more areas of their life?

---

5 Dietrich Bonhoeffer used this term in his book *The Cost of Discipleship* (New York: Macmillan, 1966).

In 1 Corinthians 5 Paul is primarily addressing a very rare case and that was of a professing Christian man having a public and ongoing sexual relationship with his stepmother under the very noses of the church leaders, elders and members. It was not being addressed, challenged or corrected. Paul's primary correction here is actually to the church and they are the ones coming under discipline for their inability to confront such a gross matter. There appears to be absolutely no sign whatsoever of repentance in this man's life. Openly and unashamedly displaying his sexually immoral relationship without a thought or care for anyone else, he was making a complete mockery of the grace message and corrupting the church with his wilful sin. This was not a man who had been struggling with lust, watching porn, even falling into adultery and through confession or exposure (King David was exposed; he never confessed, see 2 Samuel 11-12) found brokenness and grief over his sin.

This doesn't seem to be a man who had been wrestling against it, praying against it, fasting over it, asking friends and even leaders for help and trying daily to 'live holy'. This was an arrogant man, an unlawful man, a very deceived man and one that clearly disregarded what happened on the cross; a man who had come to believe that no matter what he did he was 'untouchable' and could carry on living anyway he chose.

I am aware that not all of those reading this book will be Christians, but I urge you to see sin as the very reason Jesus died for you, and His grace – His freely given, unearned favour – as the only way to inherit eternal life.

What we read here in the Bible is like a man who happily watches pornography, speaks about it openly, has no shame or remorse, and is in complete denial as to the seriousness of the sin. 1 Corinthians 5:11 tells us that we should not fellowship with a sexually immoral, unrepentant Christian. However, even in that case, hope, faith, desire and compassion must be had for this erring brother (or sister). The overriding passion should be to see restoration – which could take weeks, months or years, depending on the heart and character of the person involved. If in certain circumstances, due to the sensitivity of the case, or due to the person who is exposed or confessing their sin being in a position of authority, then maybe it is impossible for that person to continue leading in that particular church. But let the rest of the leaders inspire the congregation to believe for that fallen leader's full victory.

After years of praying and studying and listening to a hundred conflicting sermons from many well-respected Bible teachers and scholars, my revelation came very simply through a dream that confirmed what I believed theologically but could not really stand upon with conviction because I had heard so many leaders poorly teach what repentance was and was not. I believe a lot of damage is being done to some really good people that love God so much they would do anything for Him, but yet they still find themselves locked in a tormenting sin cycle.

Firstly, let me share the dream and what it meant to me and you can decide for yourself if you believe it to be theologically sound or not.

Dream that brought clarity to me

In the dream I was with a well-known leader who had and still has a big influence in my life. We were chatting away and we could see two young men from the church shoplifting in front of us in a local shop. We looked on, shocked, as these young men were caught red-handed, but what made me speak up was their response to being caught. Both of them began to laugh and clearly did not care one iota that they had been found out.

I turned to this leader and my exact words in the dream were: 'They are not repentant, I may still struggle but I would never laugh at sin.' And I woke up. I knew God wanted to speak to me and show me something, so after writing down the dream (my regular practice) I then waited on Him for the meaning. After a few moments I knew the Lord was giving me clarity in a very simple way regarding repentance.

Repentance is not about whether you never sin again after coming to Christ for salvation, it is about your ongoing attitude towards sin. If you can watch porn and then laugh about it I guarantee there is no repentance in you. You are in a very desperate place. I never once laughed about my sin, I never once denied it was sin (I did, however, deny the full extent of it – shame), but if you ask me how I felt about it I can assure you and say with conviction that I was always in a state of brokenness and despair and regret, and desperate for freedom. I continually cried out to God and I believe passionately that God knew I was repentant, yet still bound by a spiritual oppression.

I cannot blame the Church, I cannot deny responsibility, but I can now focus my fight against the real enemy in my life and stop wasting my time judging and feeling sorry for myself. I can definitely shake off the opinion of man. So can you. You know how you feel about your sin and so does God. If you are laughing about it or have convinced yourself it's OK to sin, then I urge you to wake up and stop what you are doing and ask God for the baptism of repentance in your life.

If you know you are grieving over failed attempts to be free, and you crave that freedom and have wrestled and toiled for it, then receive a gift you do not deserve: *Full forgiveness and the green light from God Himself to enjoy sweet fellowship and intimacy with Him.*

The Lord cleared up in my mind any confusion I had surrounding true repentance. Have you, like me, had it portrayed as something that you are only when you never commit that same sin again – you cannot possibly be truly repentant if you commit that same sin after you have repented? Such poor teaching and a lack of mercy is crippling so many people, especially those under a burden and spiritual oppression of sex addiction and lust. If you watch porn, or sext[6] someone, or have an affair, or steal something, or lie, or lose your temper, or... then you can laugh about it, how on earth can you say you have repented of that sin? How can you dare stand before God or man and think for a second that you should not be disciplined and face the consequences of your sin within the church government?

---

6 Engaging in sexually explicit messages or sending sexual photographs using a mobile phone/computer.

Church leaders must confront these types of cases and quickly (firstly ensuring the person is actually born again – see John 3), but I would say the vast majority of those saints that are still sinning would never laugh at what they have just done; quite the opposite, in fact. They are grieving daily over their sin and their shame, they are broken, desperate, lost and confused and they hate their sin and long for freedom. But something drives them on anyway and they find themselves in a vicious cycle of defeat.

How on earth can the Church say they are not repentant or at least remorseful and working towards a deeper repentance (which is a lifelong experience)? OK, maybe they did not come clean immediately and maybe they lied, maybe they denied, but look for the grief. Lying is not to be overlooked, I am just encouraging us to see beyond it, as shame often pushes people to lie (still wrong and still sin) and they may need some time to reflect on it all days or weeks after the fallout. Look for the brokenness, look for the desire to change and carefully navigate around the rest of the 'mess' and 'fallout' that comes in these people's lives.

Shame is so powerful in its ability to confuse both the one sinning and those dealing with it. I am not just talking from my own experiences but so many others I have spoken to, interviewed, listened to etc.

Speak life and faith into the situation and be the first to cheer these people on when they do have a breakthrough and God does His thing again in their lives! Champion their cause, do not stifle it. War for them in prayer and refuse gossip and slander and negative comments to be spoken. 'Love covers over a multitude of sins' (1 Peter 4:8, NIV) and so we must be covered if we are in sin, or cover the one who is in sin, if we find ourselves in that uncomfortable place of dealing with someone else (although we need to be careful, Galatians 6:1). Grieve with them as they grieve, pray for them and celebrate their victories and progress. Of course, in some cases there are a number of people to consider and it is not a 'normal case', which is why I am a huge advocate of handling each situation on its own merit and with much thought and prayer and time to let God work in all involved.

There is most certainly a place for discipline and restoration and each case may be very different and so cannot be approached with a 'principle' mentality but rather a Holy Spirit-led one. If you are facing the need to discipline or walk with someone through an addiction or weakness in this area, then I urge you to do so with much prayer and fasting; wait upon the Lord and ask for His heart and vision for the person or persons that you are walking with.

Remember there is a famous saying 'Only fools rush in …'[7] – I believe some sin because they have a hard heart and are full of pride and a deadened conscience, and they really may need a firm word and a 'final warning'. But, many, many people out there are locked in a cage of despair because despite crying out to God and reading their Bible more and praying and fasting and doing all the things they know to do, they are still bound. They are therefore confused and discouraged and need a loving, helping hand up. Their sin is a result of a hurt heart, not necessarily a hard heart.

---

7 Alexander Pope, 'Fools rush in where angels fear to tread.' See his poem 'An Essay on Criticism' (1711).

When dealing with a person in this sin cycle, it is helpful to look at their whole life in God before perhaps advising them that they need to take a year out of ministry, or they need to tick a hundred boxes before their repentance is proven. We need to ask them some questions about their childhood, about their current sex life with their spouse or, if they are single, has anyone in the church ever really taught them about the challenges they will face purely on a physical level? Let's get involved with a caring, loving desire to see them flourishing and enjoying the sweet fellowship of the Lord in their lives.

One of the worst things I believe that church leaders can do is continually speak to the one trapped as if they have a weak character. Firstly, I would ask a leader that shames someone that way to find an example in the Scriptures where Jesus or Paul, or one of the epistle writers in the New Testament, ever condemned a person's character. This creates such a deep shame in their life, especially when coming from someone who has influence and authority in their life.

It took a very clear word to me from the Holy Spirit to set me free from that kind of 'spiritual correction' and He did not lie to me with false encouragement and make everything seem like it was OK. The Lord also spoke to me about my character, and what He said had His discipline and grace in it. He said to me: 'You do not have a weak character, son, you have a weakness in your character.' I knew I was being challenged to address the weakness but at the same time God was removing the lie from the enemy that suggested my whole character was weak.

In the Old Testament, we read of the prophet Elijah. He was on fire for God one minute and the next he was hiding from a woman in a cave feeling depressed and defeated (see 1 Kings 19). God never spoke to Elijah like this: 'Elijah, you are full of prophetic anointing and gifting but you have a weak character!' which is really saying to that person whom God loves: 'You are a weak person!' which crushes and wounds their soul. God spoke to him in such a way that he rose back up, broke through his moment of depression and fear and stepped back into his destiny to chase down the enemies of God.

I want you to be free! I am telling you that you are not weak (look at how God dealt with Gideon in his weak area – see Judges 6!), but you may have a very real weakness that is deep-set and needs healing, renewing, freeing and filling with truth and love and authority in Jesus.

I remember only too well in the height of my own battle with sex addiction how God sent many prophetic people to encourage me. I was preaching and seeing God touch many lives but still desperately struggling with sin. So many people would come to me before, after or even during a service. and prophesy such life to me.

I was simply going on in ministry out of my gifting because that's all I really had left to lean on, or so I thought. I was desperate for freedom. I would smash phones, or block internet access, or spend much time fasting and pleading with God for freedom, but it never seemed to come.

I even got angry with God and doubted His love for me. Yes, even after every prophetic word from all those people prophesying to me the wonderful, amazing, huge destiny that God was speaking over my life. These prophets were calling me a 'nation changer' and a 'megachurch planter' and all other manner of 'wow stuff' during the time when I was experiencing the very darkest moments behind the scenes.

My point is, was God wrong? Were they all wrong? Or were they hearing from God while they were still ignorant to my sin but God was not? God calls 'into being things that don't even exist yet' (Romans 4:17).

He knows that His call on your life is a powerful weapon to draw you out of sin and shame and into true freedom. Just ask Gideon, who felt worthless and ashamed but heard the Father calling Him a 'mighty warrior' (Judges 6:12, NIV). You are a mighty warrior. You may be a mighty warrior locked in a porn addiction situation right now, but a mighty warrior you are, regardless.

Knowing that will shock the warrior into action, whereas feeling ashamed will keep that warrior caged and hidden from the world.

The trouble with shame is when it is so deep-set it will cause you to lie, deny, hide and cover up. Then the spider's web grows larger and stronger and the feelings of hopelessness deeper and more powerful over you. When confronted you may choose to lie a little here or there because, of course, you are ashamed of your behaviour and really don't want anyone to find out just how broken you are. You don't want to lose your reputation, or your title, or ministry, and so you go on. Day in, day out, week in, week out, month in, month out, year in, year out. For me, as I have mentioned, it was over a decade of repeat failure and oh, how I cried out to God for a miracle that never seemed to come.

Are you a leader in a church, and for fear of losing your ministry or your marriage, you are hoping that if you just get yourself free 'this time', then it can all just go away? That's never really worked out to well for you so far, has it? How long has it been now? How long has this been going on? This battle, this lie in your mind that says: 'I can do this without confession'? I can do this… I can do this…

I am sorry to bring bad news, but I think if you could have, you would have by now. No, sorry, confess you must, and get help and accountability you must, but it must be with someone who is prepared to do whatever it takes to see you free. So, where does our help come from?

The good news is there are a great number of church leaders and members out there that are free, and it is those I am calling to attention right now and hopefully equipping and making ready for this harvest of souls to be set free from sexual bondage. If your first experience with confessing this sin to a leader was met with a less than loving response, then that wound, I know, is very deep and underpins the whole matter of whether you confess or not. Right?

Contact me,[8] and we will do all we can to help you in this process without shame, without judgement and without anger. Leaders of churches absolutely must address this if it is something they are trapped in. I will adopt my own model of correction, which is to tell you 'You are so much better than that!' rather than 'Do you know how evil that is?' because one disarms shame and the other empowers it.

What is the main driving point behind this book? What do I believe God desires to do through it? Why am I so excited about it? Well, I believe He wants to deliver as many as He can through testimony and revelation and the disarming of sin consciousness and the condemning effects of shame. He wants to bring you into an acute awareness of your true value to God, and so I encourage you to pray this prayer before you continue reading:

Father, as I continue reading this book, help me to see what You see when You see me!

With this prayer in mind, listen attentively to the Lord.

If you are not a Christian, I really encourage you to practise this too, and with an open mind and heart say, 'OK, Jesus, if You are real, please show me this truth too.'

Christian, it is your birthright and inheritance to walk in absolute freedom and enjoy your new nature in Christ, so do not let the devil lie to you any more and cause you to believe that you are defeated. *You are coming out gold!*

---

8 Contact details are at the back of the book.

Chapter 5: Fully Forgiven

What is forgiveness and how does it rightly affect our lives?

The Lord had to take me back to this over and over again. I thought I knew what forgiveness was. I would tell people if they asked me, "Yes, I am forgiven" but I was not even close to the truth on this subject, which makes me wonder, are you? It is a huge topic but I am going to focus on the bit about you being forgiven – fully forgiven and fully free from all the guilt and shame that not understanding your forgiveness in Christ brings. I believe this is a subject so vast and so powerful that it has the potential to unlock a global prison cell and set a generation free. Of course the whole teaching of forgiveness is very clear to us. Jesus and Scripture demands that we must forgive all who have wronged us otherwise we simply cannot receive forgiveness from God for our own sins. If you have been hurt by someone in this area or any area of your life, please ask the Lord to help you take forgiveness all the way through so there is no poison left in your heart.

When we come to Christ we do so in faith. Only faith will do. Only believing in Him and the finished work of the cross ensures we are born again and enabled to stand righteous before a holy God. Not our effort, our performance, our gifting, our education, our family upbringing; no, only through faith in Christ.

The Bible says we are saved by grace *through faith* and that is not of ourselves but it is 'the gift of God' (Ephesians 2:8, NIV). Grace is the key that unlocks the heavy iron door that separates us from God, but it is faith that turns the key and even that faith is a gift from God. Nothing we can ever do can save us, or sanctify us. It is all an undeserved gift from a loving Father. Without faith 'it would be impossible to please God' (Hebrews 11:6)

Forgiveness comes to us as we believe, and the measure we believe is the measure we understand our forgiveness in Christ. 'For as [a man] thinks within himself, so is he' (Proverbs 23:7), and so, if you do not really believe and receive the free gift of forgiveness from *all* your sins, then you are still carrying the weight of them. That means you do not know how to walk in newness of life. He did so knowing that we may never actually turn towards Him. He died for the sins of the world, all the world, including you. He was as aware then as He is now of all your failings and your issues and your inability to live a fully holy life (although you are fully holy in Him: Hebrews 10:14 explains that we are fully holy now – and yet we are still being sanctified. It is the complete work but ongoing process theology. Ephesians 1 tells us God sees us through Jesus, and Colossians 3:12 teaches us that we are now holy.). He came for you anyway and is still pursuing you regardless of any sin you may be wrestling with right now. All He wants is the right to have full access to all areas and then He can do what only He can do, and that is to complete you in Himself. There is no one who can love you like He does and there is no one qualified but Him to give you an 'access all areas' VIP pass to the holy of holies – that is, an intimate relationship with Father God – through the shed blood of His precious Son, Jesus (see Hebrews 9; 10:1-18).

If you do not believe that you are forgiven for all your sins, both past and ongoing, then you will inevitably allow the shame that is attached to your mind rob you of the deeper experiences found in Christ. You will tell yourself you cannot really engage in worship or prayer or you will only ever muster up a 'feelings-based' spiritual life rather than a deep that cries out to deep (see Psalm 42:7). Your walk with God will be on and off, backwards and forwards, up and down, and there will be no real momentum and no real passion that carries you through the dark days; just a wishful thinking and some measure of hope. But I am telling you *there is a faith that can drive you through the wreckage and a forgiveness that clears the way and a relationship with the Lord that is not tainted by shame or despair.*

We learn to simply stand before the Lord unashamed and in awe of who He is.

The trouble is as humans we are so good at trying to do things by ourselves or trying to solve the deeper issues with a works-based lifestyle. Meaning, I try to stop by doing X, Y and Z rather than trusting that the Lord has fully paid for my sins. Our attitude towards ourselves and each other is often one of part grace and part forgiveness. Rather than fully accepting the complete sacrifice of the cross, we reason in our minds that there must be something left for us to do in order to be fully forgiven. That simply is not true. The measure to which we accept we are forgiven is usually the degree to which we walk in freedom.

There is a place, of course, for works coming from faith and with a Holy Spirit-given conviction, but we must recognise the difference between partnering with God by faith and establishing strong convictions while not adopting any shame whatsoever.

The overall biblical usage of the word 'forgiveness' means to send away, divorce and remove completely. It is simple logic to suggest that if we have not accepted the forgiveness of God for *all* of our sins then those sins still have some relationship with us and therefore a voice and power. If we realise they have all been sent away and we are now divorced from them, and they have no more legal right to dominate and destroy, then we can begin to walk in our new authority (and that must be exercised by faith).

Satan and sin operate outside of reason and moral fairness. John 10:10 teaches us exactly what Satan is like – he is a thief first and foremost. He comes to steal… and last time I checked it is not possible to steal something from someone if they do not already have it? The reason he can steal joy from you is because God has already given you joy when you were transferred into His kingdom. Satan cannot take your authority except by stealing it and deceiving you, even to believing that you don't already have it. An old friend of mine was a very good shoplifter simply because of his audacity. He would walk into a supermarket and pick up a case of beer and start heading for the door, stopping only to ask the security guard the time before continuing on his unashamed walk out of the exit. It usually always worked because no one was expecting a thief to just be so blatant. Satan is like that, he will steal from under our noses because we are usually so ignorant of what he is up to, and only realise when it's too late.

Maybe you can already start to see that your conviction of living a holy life by faith has been stolen from you and you now compromise more and more with less and less concern? While I certainly do not want to enable any shame access to your life, I also do not want to permit a cheap attitude towards grace. *Establish strong convictions without adopting any shame.*

God has sent your sins away 'as far as the east is from the west' (Psalm 103:12, NIV) and they no longer have the right to remain in your life. He has done it all and we now have to learn to walk in it. All the victory and all the blessing and all the authority. This is a process of maturity and growing in relationship every day.

I can imagine that in your thought life there is a constant driver that says: 'But I have to do *this* if I am to really be forgiven?' No, you don't. The only thing you have to do, and in fact the only thing you can do, is to accept and receive that He has and does and will continue to forgive you for every minor and major sin. A true lover of Jesus would never see this as a licence to keep on sinning.

We never ever deserve to be forgiven for even the little white lies, let alone the gross adulterous affairs that ravage a family and wound so many people, but He forgives nonetheless, because it is His character and His power plan to set a world free of the power of sin. Remember, God does not just forgive you out of pity, but also out of a powerful strategy to equip you to walk in new life and overcome the temptations around you.

He is the General of a precious army. You belong to the army of the Lord. He equips you through forgiveness so you can walk right and ready before Him.

If you only receive a part forgiveness and continue trying to earn the remaining portion of grace, then you'll spend a long time in misery and ultimately, defeat. 1 John 1:9 says He is '*faithful to forgive*' and 'cleanse us from all *unrighteousness*' (my emphasis).

Notice that He does not just forgive you but leave you to deal with the filth and shame and consequences of your actions. He thoroughly purges all of it, and by His own written word we are clean of the very stain of that particular sin.

The Father has fully forgiven you and the Holy Spirit has fully cleansed you and God is faithful to continue that process in your life until the day you die and join Him in glory. He does not leave you empty-handed or ill-equipped or without hope. He does not leave you alone, discarded and with commands to fend for yourself and sort it all out before you can be accepted again.

His heart is towards you, and if you refuse to hide and refuse to stop pressing in to a relationship with Him that is honest and real, regardless of where you are at, He is faithful to forgive you and cleanse you. He can and will bring you through it all. Not even the grossest and darkest porn addiction or multiple affairs can stop God forgiving you if you confess your sin to Him and bring your life exactly as it is to His throne of grace. But remember, He will never force you to enter or drag you into grace. It is all by faith and that demands action from us all. We must at the very least choose to surrender.

Just because you are working for God does not mean you are walking with God. He would much rather you were walking with Him during your battle with addiction than doing everything you can to better yourself and serve Him until you collapse and He finally gets the opportunity to minister to you.

Forgiveness is a free gift! Impossible to earn and impossible to deserve. It is completely unachievable by works and religious duty. It is a free gift that God set in His eternal plan to redeem His beloved people. I felt the Lord tell me recently He wanted to set me like a watchman on the walls of this generation and help people to see shame as it is approaching, and to sound the alarm, calling people back to grace and mercy and forgiveness. Those are our weapons of warfare, and not to be taken lightly. We wage war from this place and it is not a cheap 'sin as much as you like' message I am bringing, but a powerful deliverance from condemnation and shame so God's people can stand up straight again and live to the fullness for which Christ died.

The great Christian preacher and author, Watchman Nee presented a powerful picture of this. In his book *The Normal Christian Life*,[9] we read about a man who went to buy his wife some perfume. The man paid the asking price and received a receipt for his purchase and then lovingly gave this expensive gift to his beloved wife. She opened the wrapping and rejoiced as she saw it. After applying some to her body she got up and went to the store and tried to pay for it again. How would her husband feel, knowing he had already worked hard and paid the full price and given his wife this

---

9 Eastbourne: Kingsway, 2005.

perfume as a free gift? Why do we try to pay for something that has already been paid for? I guess it is so deeply ingrained in our thinking that we cannot fully accept the grace of God? The gift of God? The forgiveness of God? But we must.

One thing I know is that the more I accepted His forgiveness and the more I denied shame any access in my life, despite doing some utterly abominable things as a Christian, the less I would fall into the same sin. When I engaged my new thinking and put it into practice and refused to let shame have a place in my heart, I found I could engage immediately in worship and enjoy His presence regardless of my failings, and although I would always offer up a prayer of 'God, what do You want to say about this sin?' He would rarely, if ever, speak about it. He would take me rather to Scripture or give me a vision about how He sees me, or how He has called me – and I could not work out why! I was so used to having to wrestle past the shame that I had forgotten how to just accept that He really is faithful to forgive. My Father would take me to the real issues, which in my opinion is never actually the drug of choice, but the deeper issues like rejection, shame, woundedness etc.

I noticed once when reading Exodus that when Pharaoh oppressed the Israelites more severely, they multiplied (see Exodus 1:12). Could it be that due to their oppression they were having more 'comfort sex'? Could it be that drugs of every kind are much more about covering up a deeper issue or trying to numb the pain? Well, I think the secular world and the Church world would largely agree this is true, but what about porn and sexting and the like?

Are pastors recognising that some of their people are hooked on porn because they are trying to escape pain in their heart? Do they recognise that to empower them to move away from the images online they may need to stop 'disciplining a naughty child' and speak lovingly to a hurting one? I am not saying it does not involve a measure of correction but I am challenging how that correction is handled.

My spiritual father and ministry covering comes from a man called Ken Gott who I greatly admire. Apostle Ken Gott was in my life from the real early years, and due to some pride on my part, we drifted apart. Ken took me and Lydia for a meal in London a few years ago when I was in a very broken place. He told me how God had spoken to him, saying that he wasn't to deal with me as God was dealing with me Himself. He was just to let me know I was not being put on the scrap heap and God still had a powerful plan for my life. I wept as he said all this because the truth is, I did feel I was on the scrap heap! As someone once said: 'With a father failure is never final.'10

The true apostles of our generation must become the fathers this world needs, fathers that cry out 'You are not on the scrap heap!' so many arise again and become all they were created to be. Please can we ensure that no matter what the sin is we agree that the way forward is into the presence of God and relationship

10 From a tweet by Paul Manwaring who was quoting someone else – original source unknown.

with Jesus? Not a step back into legalism and works? Of course, if that person is openly in sin and carries no concern for that, then a greater challenge and discipline is required, as we've discussed.

Take them all to the forgiveness of God and if there is a time of stepping down from ministry (in severe cases), let the forgiveness of God and the restoration of God and the love of the Church rule every time. Do all you can to empower someone else towards His presence based on grace. Let's not weigh them down with religious expectations that cannot be met. If religious standards could have been met, they would have been, by the vast majority of victims.

Wow, even that word 'victim' made some of you cringe? Yes, victim! Ask a heroin addict for his story and if you listen carefully you'll soon agree that they are usually a victim of a very tragic life that would have turned the majority of us to the same escapism. Porn/sex/sexting/etc. is a drug to so many and we need to appropriate the right medication – love, forgiveness, grace, faith – to see healing come.

Maybe you are asking the question right now: 'Can God forgive me?' Well, before I even hear what you have done, or how many times you have done it, the answer is: 'Yes He can and yes He does and yes He already has.' He is passionately awaiting for you to believe it and receive it by faith. No amount of self-judgement will ever right the wrongs, no amount of striving and performing can better you as a person. Only accepting His full sacrifice on the cross can do that.

One of the words God gave me concerning my ministry when I was in Malawi recently was: 'They are largely ignorant to the real gospel.' Repeatedly preaching and teaching the gospel in Malawi, I had to go deeper in my own understanding of it. It is having a profound impact in my life. I love God so much more, I feel so much less shame, I have more passion and purpose. I am seeing incredible fruit and increased anointing and I am sinning a whole lot less. I am breaking through into amazing realms of prayer and intimacy. If I sin, I confess my sin to God, who is faithful to forgive me and cleanse me, and I refuse to accept any shame. Shame always kick-started a sexting binge and it would be days before I could manage to get myself out of it, which inevitably meant I would soon be back into it because I could not get free that way and neither can you. Ever. Period. So stop it!

I encourage you to spend some time now looking at this topic of forgiveness. Spend at least an hour or so in personal prayer, if you can. Reflect on what you just have read, and more importantly, look at what the Bible has to offer on this glorious subject. Get a Bible concordance or search on www.biblegateway.com – 'forgiveness'.

I am deeply convicted that you as a reader do not approach this book as a self-help tool but rather an inspiration into a deeper discovery of God and the freedom He offers. Read Psalm 103:1-5 as a starting point but take the time to invest in your own journey and ask God to speak to you personally about His forgiveness and what that means for you. Many times the Bible says 'Selah' after a portion of scripture, which means to 'pause and ponder'.11 If I can get you pondering, I can help you far more than if I was writing down a series of steps to victory. In reality this doesn't work. Sorry to burst that bubble, but we have to seek God and His truth for ourselves. Then it is more liberating as it brings a personal conviction from the Holy Spirit.

Pray:

God, as I position myself now in an undistracted and attentive devotion towards You, please show me this forgiveness and what it means for me personally.

11 https://selahcenter.org/selah-means/ (accessed 18.10.18).

Chapter 6: Some for Honour

Flee the evil desires of youth and pursue righteousness, faith, love and peace, along with those who call on the Lord out of a pure heart. (2 Timothy 2:22, NIV)

I cannot begin to explain just how passionately the Holy Spirit has pursued me over the last two years with this verse. Only my wife could witness to it. It has been highlighted to me literally everywhere I have gone and become a standing joke between Lydia and me.

It's like God wanted me to really, really pay attention to this verse and understand its meaning. In light of this book's theme and my own personal journey on freedom from shame, I believe it is a key verse and worthy of some attention right now. There is a wealth of empowerment in this passage and I pray now that you will discover it and more faith will arise in your heart for your current battle.

I want to draw your attention away from what you feel about yourself and more closely towards what God feels about you. Otherwise you will continue to wrestle against the flesh in the flesh, and not in the Spirit. This is where it gets more serious for the non-believer because I genuinely believe that overcoming addiction fully and walking in total freedom is absolutely impossible outside of a relationship with the Holy Spirit. You may get free in one area but more bound in another. True freedom comes only through Jesus (see John 8:36; Romans 8:1-4).

Yes, we are told to run away from 'lusts' (which is certainly not just sexual), but the Lord's wisdom in obeying this command is found here – 'pursue righteousness, faith, love and peace, along with those who call on the Lord out of a pure heart' (my emphasis). You already have a pure heart if you have repented and believed in God. I believe the victory is found in the 'calling on the Lord' (or crying out) with a passion and hunger.

The desire to live out of your inherited righteousness overrides your desire to live in the fleeting pleasures of sin. How aggressively are you crying out to God and pursuing His presence and His purpose for your life? I can assure you that a half-hearted attempt at fulfilling the dreams He has in store for you will guarantee constant repeat failure.

We have been created to be vessels for honour and of honour (see 2 Timothy 2:20-21, NKJV). We cannot sit back while the devil and this world tells us it's OK to live compromised and weak lives. Knowing I was designed by God to live an honourable life, a powerful life and to enjoy the purity of heaven empowers me. I am taking some license here to use this chapter to paint a picture of how we must see ourselves and think about being a vessel of honour, not a vessel for dishonour. The gold (noble) is how the

Father sees us but if we see ourselves as less than that we will certainly empower the shame and therefore the sin. Invite the Lord to draw your thoughts towards being the gold, honourable, precious vessel of honour that He died to restore.

In His infinite wisdom, creative genius, incredible foresight and preordained purpose Almighty God chose to form and fashion Robert Joy – He chose to form you – in His image (see Genesis 1:26-27) and therefore more valuable and more precious to Him than a billion gold bars. This truth is far more likely to get men like me out of an insignificant addiction than screaming at us 'porn is dirty, stop it'. And so the reason we stop it cannot be just because it is wrong (which it is) but because He (Jesus) has already made us right with God. Primarily I believe we turn to porn and other sexual sins because we feel devalued and we do not see ourselves the way He does. This actually helps those who have been or feel betrayed to understand more that it isn't actually a personal attack on them, but it goes much deeper than that. It is about how we see ourselves and the value we have in ourselves. Sadly, though, if I devalue myself then I only know how to devalue others. Only by seeing myself as He sees me can I begin to see you how He does too. This is critical in the healing of sexual sins, betrayal and this global epidemic. We are enticed away from our true identity because we have not really understood just who we belong to now and the lengths He went to win our hearts back to His own.

The Song of Songs – read it in The Passion Translation (TPT) – is my highest recommendation to you right now.

The reason I flee from lust and pursue Him is primarily because

I believe He is more worthy and more pleasurable and more awesome than any other desire could possibly be. When this combines with knowing that I am created in His image, and that I must therefore also be more worthy, valuable, and awesome than any other desire I may be drawn towards, then temptation starts to lose its power in the light of knowing Him.

In short, I wholeheartedly believe He is worthy of the wrestling I may have to do against such a predatory sin. Any wrestling on our behalf must be driven by desire and devotion for His presence.

Please hear me, while having a firm faith in such a radical explosive deliverance from addiction (or any sin), there is a clear scriptural precedence for the ongoing work of God over a process of time. Just because you have been trapped for years, even decades, this does not mean you are staying trapped. It is God's desire and God's pleasure that you be set free and enjoy the freedom He gives. Believe for a miracle – but also the ongoing work over time: 'I'm fully convinced that the One who began this glorious work in you will faithfully continue the process of maturing you and will put his finishing touches to it until the unveiling of our Lord Jesus Christ!' (Philippians 1:6).

The question the Holy Spirit asked me when the idea for this book first stirred in my spirit was 'Would pure gold ever chose to return to its dross?' which seemed like an usual question at first, but as the conversation unfolded and the revelation began to flow, I realised that God was trying to get me to see my value in Him. I am pure gold to God because His blood killed off all the dross and made me a brand-new creation in Christ Jesus (see 2 Corinthians

5:17). The more I believe I am dross (impurities) free and I have been made pure, then I find the scheming, cunning, deceptive and outright counterfeit temptation to return to the dross (porn etc.) less and less tempting.

I am not overcoming by fighting against it; that never ever worked. I am overcoming by believing I am better than that and my new nature is worth guarding from sin. But, more so because I believe Jesus is better than that and He is worth obeying. 'For as [a man] thinks within himself, so is he' (Proverbs 23:7), right? So think you are dirty and you'll no doubt end up in a slimy pit, but believe you are the righteousness of Christ (see 2 Corinthians 5:21) and you'll end up living like a royal heir to the throne. The journey from one to the other is different for us all, but I am determined that my testimony and this book will somehow speed up the process for you as you journey from the pit to the palace. Just promise me that when you get there, and even while on your way, you will do all you can to rescue others from the pit – because you can certainly be used by God on your way; He never uses 'perfect' people! God is not looking for polished and professional but humble and hungry.

I am an honourable vessel, and so I keep myself clean. You may feel like you are dishonourable vessel and so you end up doing dishonourable things. But thank God for the grace you now have through Jesus to live a clean life. 'How do I cleanse myself?' you say. Well, the Bible makes that crystal clear doesn't it? If you confess your sins to God then He is faithful and just to forgive your sins and cleanse you from all unrighteousness (see 1 John 1:9), meaning exactly that. You do not have to jump through hoops, you do not have to spend extended periods of time in shame and isolation, you do not have to be removed from the church and rejected by men, you just have to believe that you are forgiven and clean and loved and valued, and to hell with the devil.

How do you see yourself? A vessel for honour or a vessel for dishonour? You will always live out what you believe so choose your answer carefully.

Remember, shame brings division and so it robs us of the blessing and command of God to 'pursue … with those who call on the Lord out of a pure heart'. We all need others. We were created that way. That is why shame really must be dethroned and dismembered and cast out of our minds and our churches in Jesus' name.

I cannot win this battle by myself, with all the good will in the world and all the prayer and Bible study I can possibly muster. God has chosen in His wisdom that we run this race together, not alone. You and I both know just how brutal our enemy is and how ruthless the pull towards porn and sexual sin is, once you have tasted it; how it just keeps calling you back to its prison cell. To keep us all humble, God often gives the key to your cell door to someone else, which means you need to be teachable and vulnerable and recognise you need help. And someone else needs your help. Now, I am not suggesting that Jesus has not completely won back the key to your prison all by Himself – in truth, you need look nowhere else except to Him. We do not need to look to anyone else, or read any other book than His Word, or listen to any sermon or attend any particular church. But we are not to 'neglect meeting together' (Hebrews 10:25); He has ordained that we do. His work in our lives is often released through the ministers and ministry gifts that He has given to someone else. Read Ephesians 4!

The Church must become a safe place for all people, regardless of how broken in any area of their life they may be, so they can be confident they can confess all, receive love and mercy and ongoing relational accountability and encouragement to walk free and whole. In my own experience of the Church, that is not always the case, in the lives of those I have interviewed it is not the case, and so something must change now and change fast. Someone has to be a voice, and maybe that someone is you?

Pray:

Holy Spirit, You are the master of freedom. You love nothing more than to glorify Jesus through a transformed life. I believe You were sent to this earth primarily for my salvation and the salvation of the world; so that I could enjoy the intimacy and reality of a life filled with God. In Jesus' name I renounce all shame, and pray that You would seal that truth in my heart now.

Father, help me to see the glorious new spirit you have given me and how I can walk more freely with a new heart and new mind according to the fullness of Christ in me. Teach me how to build my faith and understanding of the new creation according to 2 Corinthians 5:17.

Chapter 7: The Wheels Are Turning

The truth is, sin destroys lives and it has a profound impact on everyone around us. *Only through repentance can we escape the invisible pull towards an eternal hell.* Our soul is ensnared and bound towards a lost eternity. Sin perverts everything about our being, and pride (the mother of all sin) cripples our ability to see reality. Satan cannot be everywhere at once and so all he has to do is what I call 'get the wheels turning' and then continue his evil desire to destroy as many lives as he can while he still has a chance. This is true of all sin and all sinners, but I am addressing primarily the sexual sins (of which there are many), which come from the root of fornication (sex outside of marriage).

The devil knows that if he can get the wheels of sexual immorality turning in your mind at a young age he has the greatest chance of keeping you locked up for an eternity. Underplaying the devil's involvement in this is one of the greatest weaknesses of the world, and a great ignorance too. Being addicted to porn or sexting etc. does not mean you are possessed, but you most certainly are under a very heavy oppression. You need deliverance from that. You need your mind to be healed; your soul that has been tormented for so long does not just 'fix itself' with a few fancy 'repeat this prayer after me' moments or self-help books or even counselling alone.

In my view, just encouraging people to repent by repeating a prayer completely misses the mark. It does not work. It actually empowers the shame because when they sincerely pray that prayer (like the majority have not prayed it a thousand times before after shutting down their porn sites for the night!) and then a few hours later, or a day or two at most, are clicking that same old site again, the enemy jumps right back in their head telling them how much of a fraud they are. Calling them a hypocrite means more judgement is heaped back on them.

I mentioned King David earlier. The Bible tells us he was a man after God's heart (see 1 Samuel 13:14; Acts 13:22) but he was not a man without sin or without a sin cycle. Just because the Bible does not record whether he ever committed sexual sin again after Bethsheba (see 2 Samuel 11-12), it does record that he repeatedly failed in other areas of life and leadership. Huge consequences were felt as a result – in his family and his nation.

Repentance is not a one-time deal, it is a lifetime of growing and maturing and learning from mistakes; of drawing closer to the Holy Spirit in relationship, and understanding who we are in Christ. The Holy Spirit guides us into all truth (see John 16:13), convicts of sin and righteousness (see John 16:8) and brings forth the power of God within us to live a more holy and fruitful life. I believe that the more I realise I am in Christ, then the less I will do outside of Christ. The more I realise I am a saint (as some Bible translations call the people of God), the less I will behave like a sinner. The more I engage my spirit in passionate pursuit of God, the less time I will have to engage the flesh.

Imagine your soul is your wife, or your younger sister, or your child, and it was driving down a dark road and the car had a slow puncture. They called you up and asked your advice. Would you advise they stopped in that dark road, alone and vulnerable, got out and tried to find the problem in the dark before continuing on their journey? Or, would you advise them to keep driving, find the nearest garage or a well-lit area so they were not only safer, but finding the problem in the light would be a whole lot easier? Would you explain that it would be less stressful and there would be less likelihood of them being hurt? We need to get hurting souls into the safest place on earth, and the most well-lit areas – which should be the Lord's Church, His body of believers, here on earth.

We should encourage those addicted souls and hurting souls to find those who have been in a similar place themselves and managed to fix the puncture and are still heading down the highway of holiness with no shame in their boot and with a red-hot engine under the bonnet. I implore you not to keep stopping your car in the dark and trying to find this puncture of yours by yourself. You are risking much greater harm this way. Pull over to a well-lit and safe place and find a person or two who are so lit up themselves that they will not judge you (and if you are judged, then forgive them and move on). Do not give up hope that God has a person for you that will represent Him well and give you hope, faith and love as you learn to fix that puncture or change that tyre altogether and stop this vicious cycle in your life.

J.C. Ryle writes this in his incredible book titled *Holiness*:

> A growing soul will try to put the best construction on other
> people's conduct, and to believe all things and hope all things,
> even to the end. There is no surer mark of backsliding and
> falling off in grace than an increasing disposition to find fault,
> pick holes, and see weak points in others. Would anyone
> know if he is growing in grace? Then let him look within for
> increasing charity.[12]

Spiritual maturity is about growing in grace and seeking to
strengthen the Church, not fault-find and weaken it. There is
a serious issue in someone's heart when they believe they have
been called to constantly troubleshoot the Lord's Church and
write books and preach sermons constantly in a bid to correct the
error of others! Be on your guard against those kind of people.
Walk with those who you can see want the very best for your soul.
Sometimes that will require some correction but it must be done
in love and with restoration at the core.

We must look more closely at those dealing with this issue, and
every issue for that matter, and determine to find the good and
stop finding all the faults. Only Satan seeks to find faults as the
accuser of the Church (see Revelation 12:10). Please don't do his
job for him. Not even on yourself.

---

12. J.C. Ryle, *Holiness (Abridged): Its Nature, Hindrances, Difficulties, and Roots*
(Moody Classics) (Chicago, IL: Moody Publishers, Kindle Edition), page 174.

Isaiah 9:2 tells us that those who walked in 'darkness' saw a 'great light' (NIV). This darkness means they were walking in obscurity, misery, destruction, sorrow, wickedness and ignorance. Ignorance will keep a soul in darkness just as easily as a great sin will. Not knowing who you are and whose you are will keep you captive in your mind and therefore captive in your behaviour. We need to stop denying this issue in the Lord's Church and we need to lovingly, wisely and soberly shine a great light on this darkness, expose the shame and set the captives free.

This word 'darkness' also means 'in secret' and this is the bulk of the reason why so many are in torment right now with sexual sin. It is in secret (darkness) rather than being brought into the light. *Let's light it up, let's get it on the churches, medias, even schools' main agenda and see it all the way through, rather than just give it twenty minutes' discussion at a men's breakfast!*

I am sounding a clarion call to the Church and inviting leaders, politicians, newspapers, chat shows, YouTubers, Facebookers, tweeters and alike to face this issue. Stop being so ignorant to it and recognise the heart of the Father who longs to see His people go free.

I spent a decade looking for a puncture in my soul while hiding in the dark and it was a lonely, scary and dangerous road. Thank God for the Mike and Heather Parkyns and the Matt and Cate Halls and the Iain and Wendy Leggetts (my in-laws) and many others that God places in our lives who know how to encourage someone to pull over at the right place and get the right attention. Do not fight the flesh in the darkness because you will never win.

Pull into the light, let it reveal the punctures in your heart and let the Holy Spirit fill those places with Himself. Shame keeps you on a dark road all by yourself and that is a set-up. Get to a well-lit area right now and find a well-lit person who carries grace and truth, and pour it out in a safe environment. Churches, leaders, please be a safe placer and a well-lit area for the Lord to direct His beautiful and much-loved kids towards so they can have their puncture fixed, or tyre changed, and stop the wheels of defeat from turning and driving them towards certain failure!

True repentance is about the transforming of the mind resulting in a change of behaviour. So, I understand why many leaders assume the position that if a person had truly repented then they would no longer repeat the behaviour. But repentance is an immediate work in the spirit but an ongoing work in the natural. It takes time for the Lord to work the full effects of the cross and Christ's victory into our hearts and minds. For me, ultimately, repentance begins with a change of mind. Do you now recognise and believe in your mind that porn is wrong? A sin? Do you believe that God wants you free of it and to stop the cycle and pattern in your life? Then I would suggest that is a sign of repentance and God is pleased to work with you.

Remember in my dream the two young men laughed and clearly did not believe they were doing anything wrong? The man in 1 Corinthians 5 openly and unashamedly having sexual relations with his stepmother and displaying no sign of repentance? That is why Paul was so quick to remove him from the church because what he was doing would affect other people. We do not see churches or the media throwing members out of fellowship for repeatedly doubting God, do we? Well, Roman 14:23 says that 'anything we do that doesn't spring from faith is, by definition, sinful' and so why do we not dismember all the God doubters that sit in our pews rather than try to get them to believe God is worthy of full passion and we can trust him fully? To do so would be absurd. We must restore not reject.

If they profess Christ (or not) and you can see that despite repeatedly giving into sin's tempting ways (even if it is a thousand times) they are remorseful, ashamed, willing to walk with someone on the journey into freedom, then give them full support and love and care. Relationally and prayerfully let them know you are fully serving them, and even if that means a time out of public ministry or media attention you will do everything you can to see the victory of Jesus worked out in their life.

I sat in a meeting last year as Isobel Allum, an internationally renowned prophetess, was sharing a testimony of this issue. A man had visited their local church and told them how he had been removed from every church in the area due to gross sexual immorality. She alluded to it being sexual sin and it was clearly a deeply immoral case. This man came to see Isobel and her husband, Ivan, because years before they had visited a church this man was attending and prophesied over him a wonderful vision God had for his life. However, after they finished and left the church, this man was pulled into the church leader's office and because they knew his history and all his many failings, the leaders told him that Isobel must have got it wrong. The life-giving word from a Father in heaven that has the ability to see beyond the sin and into the potential of us all was stolen from this man by those in authority.

Years later and this man was at his wits' end and had attempted suicide several times. He was a fornicator, an adulterer, addicted to all kinds of porn and was regularly sleeping with prostitutes, yet God had apparently spoken a powerful prophetic word over his life. After deciding to visit Isobel and Ivan to ask them if they felt they had missed it and prophesied over the wrong man, the prophetess and her husband decided to get involved. Local church leaders called them up and warned them to have nothing more to do with him. These two Spirit-filled saints had the courage and the grace to take on all this persecution and continued to love and support this gross sex addict. They put steps in place to minimise risk, which is wise, and they moved him into their own home. They had him type up the prophecy and read it several times a day and listen to it on audio several times a day. This went on for weeks and was certainly not without heartache. Several times he went off to find a prostitute, and many times he lied and let them down and many times people said, 'I told you so.' They had to repeatedly talk him out of suicide and could see how broken and hurt this man was. But they chose to love him and risk it all because they could see in him a glimmer of repentance and a man who seemed to genuinely want freedom.

Well, after months of working with this man, he found himself totally free of sexual immorality. More time went by and he met and married a wonderful woman. More time went by and

God started to exalt him and his testimony and now he travels the world as a powerful weapon of grace and hope and teaches others too.

Isn't that just incredible? What a glorious reward awaits Ivan and Isobel Allum in heaven for seeing through the eyes and hearing through the ears of Jesus and recognising that this man was not all evil, but broken and alone and had been discarded by so many, but not by Jesus.

How would the majority of us handle that situation? Would that man be free today and empowering thousands of others? Or would he still be dismembered and discarded, or dead from suicide? They saw something in him and prophetically and *repeatedly* called it out of him until he saw it too and the fullness of repentance permeated his mind and changed his behaviour. Awesome!

Now in my experience and in the lives of some of those I have been walking with recently, it is certainly not common for people to view cases like the man I have just mentioned the same way the Allums did. They saw something and heard from God concerning His purpose for this man and they walked with him through the filth of it all until the freedom truly came. This is not intended to shame the Church but simply to encourage us to prepare to get messy and get involved on a deeper level as it certainly takes more than a couple of meetings designed to bring 'correction' and discipline. But we must be wise and use safety measures when dealing with this sin, more so, I believe, than any other.

Let me share with you a couple of very powerful dreams I believe God gave me recently that He wants me to share and interpret as a way of helping many of His well-loved but addicted children.

Pray now that God would enlighten you to see in these dreams His prophetic, intentional desire to deliver you and stop the wheels of shame and defeat from turning. In Jesus' name.

Chapter 8: Level 5 Grace

I was in a car park that had many levels to it and I was looking for a group of people that I believed could help me. I thought they were on level 4 and so I got off the lift at this level only to find this level had three people (one of them was a pretty woman who was very exuberant and quite distracting) and they clearly wanted to have a fight and cause destruction. I then realised that my helpers were not on level 4 but in fact they were up on *level 5*.

Suddenly there was an open battle between level 4 and level 5 and I was getting caught in the crossfire. I managed to get myself onto the ramp that cars would use to drive up. I stopped half way up between levels and realised I needed to get involved and fight, but I was unarmed and now in a very dangerous position.

A guy gave me a gun and I tried to get a few shots off at the people on level 4 but I was distracted by this woman who was dancing around and drawing my attention. All my shots were missing and their shots were getting closer and closer. The team up on level 5 were safely out of reach from those on level 4 and they were in a very comfortable position, but they could see I was in great danger. As this dancing girl was distracting me I didn't notice one of the men she was with sneaking up behind me until it was too late. I turned just in time to see him aim his gun and shoot at me from close range.

The dream was extremely detailed and felt so real and I can still remember the feeling of the bullet going straight into my head as I was trying my best to fight back. I was powerless on this ramp that was neither level 5 nor level 4 but a kind of no man's land. The woman told me I had to stay down and get out of the fight and off they went, satisfied that another man had been taken out of the battle.

I remember the blood and the feeling I had in the dream that I was about to die of this head wound, and how something inside me rose up and an indignation took hold as my heart told me it was not my time to die. I needed to get back up.

As I tried to get back up, the people on level 5 came down to where I was and stood by me and watched encouragingly as I fought to get back on to my feet. The blood that was pouring from my head wound started to dry up and they all looked on amazed as I reached inside my own mouth and began to pull out large fragments of bullet. The fragments were full of blood and sticking to the roof of my mouth and I had to spit them out. With each fragment I removed from my mouth I was able to speak a little more clearly, and when all the fragments were gone I could speak with total clarity. I said, 'I am back in the fight' and that I needed to 'sort my weapons out' and then I woke up.

It was in the early hours and my room was very dark, with my wife asleep beside me. So I wrote the dream down and began to pray. I heard the Holy Spirit say a few things in that moment that has massively changed my mind and my confession. 'The devil tried to stop you going to the next level by having you focus your attention on the level below (my past).' As I heard this the song 'Livin' la Vida Loca' was clear in my mind. If you listen to that song, and its lyrics, this was very much how I was feeling at the time.

In the Bible the number 5 is commonly believed to be the number for grace and I was trying to find this level because I knew it was a safe place. I believe the Lord is saying that a multitude of well-meaning people that are trying their hardest to fight against lust and other distractions in their life have not yet entered this grace level. They find themselves in no man's land because they are still not living in freedom, despite great effort and willingness to fight back.

Those that are clearly positioned in grace can better see the enemy, the distractions and the threat and are so hidden out of sight and out of reach of the enemy that he cannot stop them from advancing. The enemy is not permitted onto the grace level. God is seeing the desire and the remorse of so many people that want nothing more than to overcome their enemies and distractions, but find themselves unarmed and unable to advance.

The enemy has clear sight of them and a strategy to pick them off. I believe sex addiction and all addiction, for that matter, is a brain disease. It is unseen to most. The Lord is now sending his level 5 warriors to come down and encourage those who need them the most, and show them how to advance to level 5 where the devil cannot find them. Of course, we can all still stumble regardless of knowing grace, and we must always stay awake and be aware that we are in a daily battle against a real spiritual enemy, and due diligence and daily intimacy with the Lord must be our focus. This dream is an incredible picture of grace and there are several things I feel need to be considered right now.

1. Is repentance really holding a position where we never sin again? Or is it more about the heart and the desire to overcome and walk in freedom? (Leading, of course, towards absolute freedom.)

2. Does God shame the sinner or is He more aware of the person's heart and effort to be free and responds accordingly?

3. Are you holding a secure position of grace, or are you somewhere else?

   • No man's land?

   • Or on level 4, not reaching down to help those who really do want to give God and their families their very best?

I am convinced that if the grace of God surrounds a wounded or fallen person, then the ability to remove the fragments of bullet and find our voice again (our confession of Christ) will soon come. Another son or daughter will be back in the battle using their testimony to further the kingdom of God.

I feel very strongly that God was applauding me in this dream for being someone that despite being shot at and seriously wounded in the past has never ever given up the fight. I believe that is absolutely true of you too, simply because you are reading this book right now and looking for something, anything, that might help you move into a full or fuller freedom.

I implore you to keep going and to never quit and I pray you find Jesus as the Healer. However, please make sure you have sorted out your weapons and you know from which level you should be fighting from!

Grace permits you to join those who have discovered this truth and gone before us and live in a state of victory thanks to Jesus. Get the right confession in your mouth by removing the fragments of shame and condemnation that you, Satan or others may have heaped upon you. You are back in the fight now and the weapons of your warfare 'are not carnal but mighty in God' (2 Corinthians 10:4, NKJV).

Refuse to give up the fight and stay defeated when Jesus shed His blood and took all the bullets so you and I could live on level 5, which is the position of grace and freedom.

I do not believe God gets people free by judging them and shaming them but I do believe He calls us out and seeks to draw our gaze heavenwards, even in the deepest and darkest affair with porn or adultery and the like, because He knows the real you and He knows the One inside you (if you have been born again – that is, if you have acknowledged Him as your Lord and Saviour). He is not ignorant to the you that He created and He is jealously, zealously and powerfully bringing you back to the understanding of the value you have in Him.

The very next dream I had after this one had a similar meaning. I was in a hotel and I was lost and I could not find my room. I was asking people which floor I was on. I got off at the wrong floor, ended up in the wrong room and very quickly found myself in a very inappropriate scene. I ran out of that room and then I woke up.

Immediately the temptation was to look at porn because the dream had been fairly graphic (but not gratuitous), and in the past something like that would have been more than enough to push me over the edge and into sin. However, this phrase came to my mind very powerfully: 'I do not fight to get it out of my mind, I just get my mind into the spirit.' Within a few seconds the strong temptation became a very weak one and I gained the victory. Unrepentant people do not get the victory because they are not looking for it, and so if you find yourself in a place where sometimes you win and sometimes you lose I would suggest that you are already winning because there is at least the evidence of a desire to change.

I would advise you strongly to guard your mouth. Don't allow any fragments of shame and guilt to keep you speaking negatively about yourself when God the Father does not. For me, I got to the place where I could enter into worship immediately after stumbling, falling.

I learned that the worst thing I could do if I had given into temptation was to retreat from worship and fellowship with God. The immediate love and encouragement God gave me in those moments began to correct my mind, fuel my heart and set me free. Yes, you are permitted into His grace and heart regardless of a sin cycle or ongoing battle, and it is imperative that you do so if you are to get to the grace level which, when understood, gives freedom and passion and intimacy like you will never have experienced before.

The devil and the world (and sadly, even some Christians) try to bring you down to their level, whereas godly believers and the Holy Spirit always seek to encourage you and help remove the bullets and the pain. They lead you up to level 5 where the real grace, goodness, glory and power of God is. Grace came down to rescue me and grace is here to rescue you too. What a precious Jesus we have, the lover and Saviour of our souls. Grace teaches us how to live holy lives once it (He) has come down to us (Titus 2:11-14) which is good news; you and I do not have to stay in no man's land, lost and defeated; we can and must rise up and 'live holy' by grace through faith.

I no longer spend pointless time trying my hardest (and only God knows how hard I tried) to get immoral thoughts and desires out of my mind because I learned the hard way that it is a complete waste of time and incredibly exhausting and demoralising. I engage my mind in the Spirit of God now.

If you have a mind filled with evil desire and lust and have just watched porn a few moments ago, make a decision right now to turn on some worship music and speak out some praise to God. Allow yourself the grace that if rightly understood will never give you a licence to keep on sinning but will eventually break through into your soul and mind and wake up on the inside of you a much deeper love relationship with Jesus, which is absolutely the only way to be free and stay free.

If your hands are dirty, is the best way to change that situation to spend hours staring at your hands acknowledging the dirt and hoping that they will miraculously clean themselves if you only shout hard enough or pray hard enough? Or is it not better to just grab some soap and water and clean them? Staring at your dirt will not change a thing, but appropriating the cleansing agent of the blood of Jesus and the washing of the water of His Word will (see Ephesians 5:26). Shame keeps you sin-conscious and grace moves you to being Christ-conscious.

This is the baptism of repentance that I am seeing coming to a world full of sexually addicted souls and those lost to drugs. Just preach grace and know grace and live in grace and stay on level 5.

If for some reason your heart is drawn back to level 4, do not stay there and try to fight your way out of it, confess your sin to God, who 'is faithful and just and will forgive us our sins and purify us from all unrighteousness' (1 John 1:9, NIV). Stay in grace, which is the power weapon here. Look up to grace and those on level 5 and cry out 'cover me' as you turn and run towards them and enjoy the higher life in Christ.

In my dream the people on level 5 were trying to lay down some cover fire but I felt I couldn't just turn and run. I needed to keep fighting. Honourable maybe, but it doesn't work. We need to cover and be covered by the fire of God.

It is not your time to lay down and die and leave the fight. It is your time to get to level 5 and fight from a place of assured victory in Christ.

Repentance most certainly does mean a change of behaviour and that flows out of a change of mind, but my concern is where some people assume that this behaviour change happens overnight. It certainly can, but when we are dealing with such a sensitive issue as sex addiction it can take a process of time. Sex addicts do not become addicts overnight and they generally do not stop overnight either. I am absolutely believing to see an army of addicts experience such a power encounter with God that they really are set free immediately, and I'm sure there are testimonies like that we can all celebrate together, but often it is more likely to be a journey that can take time as the Lord begins to heal, deliver and recalibrate old ways of thinking.

Our thinking must align to His own written Word so the we begin to see more clearly and are able to rationalise the truth that sets sinners free. If we picture the ideal scenario of repentance, it definitely would look like a man or woman recognising sin, confessing it to God, making a sharp 180 degree turn and never ever touching that sin again. I am 100 per cent for this and cry out to God for such radical transformations in my mind and behaviour. And I can testify to many such events. More often though, and certainly with addictive behaviours repentance can look more like a semicircle or an arch as the Holy Spirit seeks to steer the mind round to a full repentance. There can be a whole array of things that can contribute towards someone not 'getting it' straight away, and the grace we need to walk in as they journey towards freedom is critical.

The heart may have completely given itself to abstaining from porn, but the mind is so used to having its own way. Even from a medical point of view the deeply ingrained trenches that repeat porn use create in a human brain determines whether it is going to give up the fight or not. 'Every time you have a thought, it is actively changing your brain and your body – for better or for worse.'[13]

We absolutely need the grace, goodness and power of God. Jesus called 'sinners to repentance' (Luke 5:32, NIV) and it is still the work of the Lord's people today – to bring sinners to repentance, and to faith in Christ through the Holy Spirit. But the 'faith in Christ' bit is absolutely, totally vital for repentance to take full root in a soul. Faith is all about learning to trust and rely on Christ and not our own abilities and self-righteousness. Yes, repent, but repentance without faith is merely religion – ritual – without power, and can never work because it was designed not to.

Mark 2:17 really highlights this to us as Jesus explains that His purpose was (and still is) to bring sick people to repentance. We must understand that addiction of any kind is a sickness. Yes, often brought about by poor choices, but we need to go deeper than that and ask the questions why someone has turned towards heroin, cocaine, alcohol, porn or multiple affairs etc. Let's not keep brushing this under the rug but rather lift the rug up, get

---

13 Dr Caroline Leaf, *Who Switched Off My Brain?* (Southlake, TX: Inprov Limited, 2009).

the world to stop being so shocked as to the dirt that is revealed, and start praying and planning how we can best clear this awful mess up.

We need to love people back to life and bring life and liberty to another generation. Jesus recognised that in many cases sin was as a result of broken-heartedness and some form of soul disease. Sin is a disease and Jesus' blood is the cure. We must all be instruments of love and support to a dying generation.

It seems that every other day another celebrity is exposed as some kind of sexual predator, and although some are, it is a title I do not give people. Many of them are people with a disease. When a celebrity we all love comes out in the press as having a secret addiction to painkillers and alcohol we rightly rally around and cheer them on and wish them a speedy recovery. When someone comes out or is exposed as having an addiction to sex, causing a behaviour pattern in their life that is totally inappropriate and often abusive in some way, we absolutely slam them and hold them up to account.

Please understand I am not suggesting that in some cases this is not necessary to protect others, but I dare to suggest that many of these people are devastated by their own lifestyle and have tried many times to stop and made many promises and vows to do so, only to find they cannot. But of course each case must be looked at appropriately, and when someone is intentionally using their position of authority or celebrity status etc. we have to accept that the judgement is harsher and often the punishment more severe. I pray this book does fall into the hands of those in that category and the Lord uses it to bring them to their knees in repentance, and they would confess and walk through whatever is required to bring them into freedom, and their victims are properly cared for. I want to make it very clear I am never advocating a cover-up or excusing and brushing mess under the carpet. My ultimate goal in this book is to bring as many as I can towards their freedom. Those caught up in it and those negatively affected by it. 'It is for freedom that Christ has set us free' (Galatians 5:1, NIV).

We would be better placed to grieve with the genuinely repentant and listen to them and offer our non-judgmental hearts to them if we ever want to see them set free. Consider Paul's second letter to the same church that he disciplined for tolerating such a gross sexually immoral relationship. In 2 Corinthians 2, there is a view that Paul is fighting for the cause of the same man he was quick to remove from fellowship previously. Let's assume that he *is* in fact talking about the same person.

He understands that it is highly likely this man will be swallowed up with sorrow and potentially lost from fellowship forever if a quick 'love in action' is not taken up on his behalf. Maybe the Father saw this broken man alone in his room grieving over his sin but not knowing how to respond or who to believe, with all the voices contradicting each other raging inside his head. I guarantee those voices would have been there and this man was wrestling with them on a daily basis. God saw this man, God loved this man, God wanted to restore this man.

Look at verse 8: 'I urge you to reaffirm your love to him' immediately after verse 7: 'forgive and comfort him, lest [he] be swallowed up with … sorrow' (NKJV).

Take the level 5 approach and go find the ones who are hurting right now, those bleeding from head traumas and defeat, and call them to rise, and love them back to life in Jesus' name. Of course, if they reject your advances of love and forgiveness and they are proud and kick against you, then walk away. Pray, hope and believe for their moment of humility to come swiftly so they can be healed and used of God again.

I am convinced the great majority of fallen ones will take your forgiveness and underserved love as a mighty weapon against the enemy's shame on their life, and it will be used by God to see them delivered and walking right again.

This is such a massive subject and there are some compelling arguments as to what true repentance is and is not. I am speaking about this so much because I am primarily trying to get us to see that just because someone does not tick all the boxes and fulfil all the criteria that someone is 'truly repentant' does not mean they are not desperate to be so. And therefore in my opinion they immediately qualify for our time and attention. For many of them they just haven't had a breakthrough revelation on the grace of God and the full forgiveness of sin and so they operate out of an attitude that they must prove themselves and become worthy of forgiveness.

If you are going to repent, repent of that wrong thinking, change your mind about that. You may not be worthy of forgiveness, but I would definitely suggest you were worth forgiving. Your value to God (your worth) was why Jesus went to the cross in the first place.

Being 'transformed by the renewing of your mind' (Romans 12:2, NIV) is much less about knowing that sin is wrong and much more about knowing you are right now with God, thanks to Jesus. You are right with God, you are perfect in His sight and you are made whole at the cross. Focusing your attention here will ensure that your spirit man is engaged, which has an automatic effect on your thoughts towards sin. If your focus is the sin itself then you will always be fighting the flesh in the flesh. I promise you that will exhaust you, disappoint you, and leave you feeling utterly defeated and filled with shame.

We need a fresh baptism of repentance in the Church, we need our minds saturated with a conviction of sin and a conviction of our righteousness. This will bring us all into the light and into a safe place.

In Mark 1:15 Jesus begins His ministry message to the earth (the sick and the oppressed) with a sermon that could only be titled 'Repent, and believe in the gospel' (NKJV).

If you keep your eyes fixed on Jesus who is 'the author and finisher of our faith' (Hebrews 12:2, NKJV) then we have little time for anything else that seeks to destroy our destinies. The danger with porn and the like is that it has this stigma and this shame attached, and so we immediately feel that we cannot possibly come to God and worship Him until we have said sorry a thousand times, prayed through gritted teeth and tears, and spent a few days at least feeling rotten about ourselves.

I am not denying there is a biblical place for grieving over sin and being broken and contrite (see for example Psalm 51:17), absolutely yes, but it is His presence and His grace that permeates our fractured minds and wounded souls and removes the 'drivers' or 'triggers' that lead us into more darkness.

I know full well that for you to even think you could dare to engage in worship immediately after viewing porn or stepping out in some other form of sexual behaviour contrary to Scripture does not sit well with you. I am not talking about accepting porn in your life and living compromised. I am talking about a method of freedom that is working for me and was instrumental in getting the shame off so I could see clearly and re-establish my faith in Christ. I am charging you to live a 100 per cent porn-free life.

I am declaring that sexual sin is wrong and must be removed from our lives and is a very serious issue. I am sounding the alarm to my generation and the next that grace is the way. Level 5 is the way.

God delights in you while despising your sin. He loves you so deeply He is willing to do all it takes to separate you from any sin, no matter how gross it may be. He is committed to this process.

I hope this has helped somehow in drawing your mind away from shame and towards grace and look forward to your testimony and feedback!

Pray:

God, help me to recognise the difference between condemnation and conviction. Teach me to live a life well and one that responds quickly to the conviction of sin You so lovingly bring so as to continue cleansing me from all unrighteousness.

Chapter 9: Testimony and Prophecy

When my sex addiction and resulting inappropriate behaviour was brought into the light (not by confession, I am afraid to say) I suddenly had the rug pulled out from under me and my entire world went into a violent tailspin. My family and I moved out of our home and the town we had planted a church in. We had to sleep as a family on the floor in my gracious and Christ-like in-laws' home (their reaction to me was a vital part of the healing process). We lived for several weeks out of bags, and in heartbreak.

We lost friends, we lost reputation, we lost ministry and we nearly lost the will to live. We had some very good and godly people come around us, but we still felt largely alone as we wrestled with all the feelings of regret, shame, depression and failure. I say 'we' because this always affects the whole family, not just you. I managed to keep up a discipline of sorts in prayer and shutting the door and getting alone with God, but did He have to shout loud to get my attention!

Through all the screaming negative thoughts and feelings in my own mind God still managed to weave in His love and truth. I felt lost and alone, and knowing it was self-inflicted only made it worse to deal with. I had lived with this shame for so long, but because I was still getting some recognition from my spiritual peers and seeing fruit in ministry I could kind of bear it.

Now all that was gone and I had nothing but a trail of hurting people around my life as a result of my addiction. People that had looked to me for leadership now knew that I, Robert Joy, actually didn't have such a perfect life after all. I felt the weight of this so heavily on my soul. I lost sleep, found it easy to drink a glass or three of red wine at night to at least steady my nerves and could very easily, if it were not for the grace of God, taken a lot more alcohol to numb the pain.

I had really encountered Jesus in 2005 and I was about to find out that He does not give up on those who call upon His name.

I realised I was more addicted to sexting than I was porn, and I would find myself quickly overcome with temptation to text a girl sexually. The more it happened it seemed the less I was able to fight against it, and then it got to the point where I would actually look for opportunities. The devil had pulled me into a deadly trap and I was not spiritually, let alone mentally, equipped to handle this assault. I had to learn fast and I had to give myself to the Lord fully. Why did I need to hear someone tell me over a text message that I was sexy, or I was amazing?

I also believe that without dealing with the spirit realm on this issue we really are fighting a losing battle. In my case I have to say that I am convinced it was more about dealing with the spiritual side of all this, and nothing was really going to change until it changed first in the spirit.

As part of my restoration I decided to take my family to Folkestone where my sister Nichola and her family lived at the time, and just try to get away from things for a while – only to find that shame refuses to let you take a much-needed holiday and demands to share the same spot of beach with you. Shame refuses to just go away.

I dragged myself to my sister's church under some influence from my family as a visiting preacher from America was due to minister that night. As he preached on loving God I tried to glean anything I could from his message and make a bit of a comeback, but I was extremely low and my faith was very weak. I had not lost my faith in God, but I was definitely believing that I was out of action, so to speak, and I could forget about fulfilling all the prophecies over my life.

At the end of his message this preacher gave the familiar altar call for prayer, and after a long mind battle with shame that was telling me to stay in my seat and give up, I found myself walking forward anyway. I stood in a long line of people all waiting to be prayed for. I remember weeping as this man laid his hands on me and said, 'The Lord is saying that all will see the vindication of God upon your life and everything will go full circle.' I wept and wept and wept. This was the first prophetic word that God used to bring hope back to my soul and a flicker of faith awoke within me. His wife went on to say that in the parable of the prodigal son in Luke 15, the father forgave the lost son but the big brother never did. She likened this to God forgiving me but 'others' might not. I was encouraged but also gutted as the reality that my sin had caused such grave consequences set in. Although God forgave me, it did not mean that everyone would.

I managed to stay porn-free for quite a long time but mainly because I was depressed, and for once in my life seemed to have no sex drive at all. Once that changed I found that giving up porn and even sexting wasn't going to be too easy, regardless of my desire and even desperation to do so.

The Lord began to deal with both my wife and I on judgement and we repented for how we had spoken against other leaders and ministries, and gone along with those who had even publicly named other churches and groups and spoken negatively about them. We found this to be something God was firmer with us on than the actual addiction issue. It seems to us both that God really was not happy with His beloved churches and groups and leaders being judged, and He began to show us the immense blessing of drawing from the well of others, even when you do not see eye to eye on every theological point.

We had fallen into a very dangerous trap of believing that we shouldn't let anyone from outside the group we were in speak into our lives. After seeing just how poor our thinking was and how we had cut ourselves off from so much blessing, we knew we had to repent. Especially for even teaching our church to live like this. Suddenly God started to use various ministries (some we had spoken against) to pour life and healing and blessing back into us. It really was like a well was reopened that simply through repentance God used to wash over us and reaffirm to us the real calling that was on our lives.

I kept thinking about the preacher's prophecy that it would all go 'full circle' and wondered what that meant. At first I thought it might mean that we would return to the people we had so badly hurt. I confess that I dreaded the thought of that because Lydia and I now felt so strongly that we were to receive from certain ministers and ministries that they would never endorse. It was a strange time of wrestling through all of this until I heard the Lord say that 'full circle means reconnecting with Ken Gott'. Ken had first trained me and released me into ministry. I felt strongly that I needed to repent to Ken and that through this repentance God wanted to reopen a specific well in my life that I had somehow lost during a previous season.

I made a four-hour journey to Sunderland to meet Ken and Andy, an elder at Ken's church, in a hotel, had one lemonade and asked them to forgive me for judging them and not understanding them correctly. Then I asked if they would pray for me. They were both incredibly gracious and prophesied and encouraged me, and I then drove four hours back down south and climbed into bed with my sleeping wife and small children.

I may never know the full significance of that day, but suddenly the prophetic anointing on my life took on a whole new level, and words of knowledge[14] began to pour out of me. I was seeing faith and passion for Jesus increase again. Ken Gott carries a major emphasis on our primary ministry being to just stand before God. I learned to stand before God again, and with no platform to preach on, invitations to accept and people to lead, I could only

14 A gift of the Holy Spirit. See 1 Corinthians 12:8.

give myself to re-establishing a deeper relationship with the Lord. I wish I could say it was all plain sailing from then on, but it was not. There were more mistakes and the battle was intense, but through it all God would give me dream after dream, prophecy after prophecy and hope after hope. He was relentless in His efforts to win my heart and remove my shame, and the way He dealt with me was life-changing.

Lydia and I spent an evening in London with Ken Gott one day, as he was preaching near us and invited us to join him for a meal. I never got to eat much of my Chinese that night because I was too busy weeping at the table as he said a few words that poured more hope into my soul. I decided to tell Ken just how serious my issue had been and gave him a bigger picture of what I had done, and also a few things that had happened. How I would wake up to Facebook messages from girls I hadn't seen in years literally offering me sex, which I thank God I never did; random events like a drunk girl jumping into my car as I left the church one night after preaching on holiness and offering herself to me for a lift home (again, thank God I got the victory and never did).

There were many other events like that (things that never ever happened to me before I was a Christian) and as I shared all this with Ken, he sat back and said, 'Why has no one recognised yet that you are a victim in all this too? This is a demonic attack against you.'

Ken then told me how he had been at a conference recently and as an evangelist was preaching he began to think about me, and this was when he felt God say he was not to let me stay on the scrap heap and that he was not to deal with me, because God was dealing with me Himself – I have mentioned this earlier. He told me how God asked him to encourage me and invite me to travel with him at times.

It was a very powerful night and was a big game-changer in how I started to view the whole spiritual realm. I realised that by my own ignorance I had not taken spiritual warfare seriously enough and I needed to learn how to fight the devil and overcome him if I was to gain victory in the natural realm.

One day I had a WhatsApp message come from a number I did not have stored or recognise. It sounded like it might be one of my painting and decorating business customers so I replied politely, apologising that I did not know who it was. The reply shocked me; someone said they had messaged me by mistake but then saw my profile; followed immediately by several pornographic photos in quick succession of a woman.

Was it just a random chance event or was it a strategically planned attack by a real enemy? I know what I believe. I got the victory on this and I deleted the photos and the number. A few days later this same person sent a video through without warning. Once I blocked the number another number was used to send an obscene image through. Over the course of a few weeks this deliberate attack became very heavy. I told my wife and I told my friend Matt Hall and asked for prayer. These random numbers were used to invite me to local sex parties saying I would be greatly received but it was highly demoralising for a man who is fighting a serious addiction to pornography and the drive for lust.

I even woke this morning after a barrage of highly sexualised dreams (which hasn't happened in a long time) but the exciting thing is that I was immediately able to draw on the truth of what I have been writing in this book and instead of turning to porn I turned to worship and just began to write.

It is all linked together and although not all men that view porn are under a definite spiritual attack against them personally, many are. Especially leaders that Satan can see are winning souls and advancing the kingdom of God. I believe Ken Gott was right and I was experiencing a very real spiritual, demonic attack to destroy me, my marriage and my destiny.

I was in Malawi preaching last year and while I was there God broke out in an unexpected way with stunning miracles and healing and words of knowledge. It was very exciting and a powerful time of ministry. This particular trip taught me more about the devil and more about the spirit realm than any church or sermon or leader ever had. This was the school of the Holy Spirit. I was about to learn fast.

I saw many delivered from demons, including young children that had been dedicated by parents and grandparents to witchcraft. It was a great wake-up call to the reality of demonic influence in people's lives. After one particular service, they asked me to pray for a lady who seemed old and frail. As I reached out to put my hand on her head and pray, I saw her face and entire being change. She lunged wildly at me to try to bite me.

Kind of by instinct more than anything else, I shouted the name 'Jesus!' at her. Me and several bishops and many members of the church witnessed first-hand just how powerful that name is. The woman flew back at least ten feet and crashed to the hard, dirty floor. I ran over to her to cast out the demon but she jumped to her feet with strength that was not natural, and ran away. Everyone began to laugh and cheer but I did not. I was grieving that I did not get the opportunity to cast the demons out and see her restored to her right mind and the local fellowship of believers.

On my next trip to Malawi I again experienced a powerful outpouring of the Spirit and many miracles took place before my eyes. Deaf people being healed, blind people seeing, and broken bones being healed. All manner of stunning demonstrations of God's power. I was definitely now on the devil's radar as I was stepping into the real call of God on my life, which was never to pastor a church but to be a revivalist to the nations.

I found out that the devil was now really mad with me. I was experiencing a strange insomnia one night in my small lodge; while my friend slept soundly I was being tormented in my mind. After a few hours of this I decided I had to get up and take authority over this attack, and when I did so I fell asleep almost immediately.

I dreamt there were a few witches close by to where I was staying and they were sacrificing chickens and chanting curses at me. They kept saying 'Destroy him, destroy his ministry, destroy him, destroy his ministry' and the Lord gave me a word of knowledge right there, showing me there were local witches trying to disturb my sleep and ultimately take me out. I am not blaming the devil for all my mistakes, nor am I justifying them, but when is the Church going to wake up and realise that our enemy is real and he delights in destroying those whom he sees as a threat to his kingdom?

Great men of God that have fallen over the years probably did not wake up one morning and say, 'I know, I am going to sin today and throw away my reputation, my dignity, my calling and my family.' Without permitting sin in our lives and churches we must still hold to a level 5 position for the Church, which is grace and restoration and limitless love. Satan is a thief and he is a master manipulator and therefore ill-equipped churches are so easily weakened by him as he simply continues his assault on believers.

I really feel that by sharing some of my testimony and many of the prophetic words given to me by others or by God Himself directly in dreams and/or visions, there is a chance that something will jump out at you in this chapter, and give you hope. I want this book to arouse your faith to go on in the ways of God.

One dream I had was heartbreaking. I woke up in the early hours from this dream with a real sense of urgency to hurry up and finish this book. A family had been devastated by a man's infidelity and his in-laws were talking to him and loving him (just like mine did), but despite the grace they showed to him, the wife and the children were alone in another room sobbing together as their whole world was shaken by this infidelity.

I noticed how the man was genuinely sorry and had actually been coerced by a tempting younger woman (who was not evil herself but also wounded and lonely), and the whole scene really affected me.

In the dream I saw a small evil figure of a man lurking in the background of this entire mess and knew it was the devil. It was like the Holy Spirit allowed me to see that none of the people involved were evil, or hell-bent on hurting anyone else, and all were genuinely gutted that their actions had caused such great harm. We must not be ignorant of Satan's schemes (see 2 Corinthians 2:11).

Sin does have consequences and the hurt is very real, and it takes time for God to then turn darkness into light where people are concerned. Whether you are someone who was caught or someone who was hurt directly by another's actions, I pray you will know comfort and encouragement from the Lord. When I woke up and prayed I heard the Lord say to me: 'Infidelity is the biggest cause of divorce and family devastation, it is a satanic attack.'

I am not downplaying people's involvement and poor choices, but I am now absolutely convinced that God is trying to prophesy to the nations concerning this epidemic which is clearly a very real satanic attack. Despite humanity's shortcomings and failures, Satan is at the heart of it all. We must turn our attention to our real enemy, which is not each other and is not even the porn itself, or the porn industry.

It is now time to get the bullets out of the minds of God's beloved people and arm them with a right confession and understanding of who they are in Christ. We must restore the value He places on them, regardless of how filthy their behaviour. We must stop fighting each other and learn how to pull Satan down and exalt Jesus Christ in this situation. It is time for the nations to come out gold.

In my opinion, and according to many therapists, we must sort our weapons out and arm ourselves with a right mindset. My vision here is to deal more with the spiritual realm and offer some revelations that called me out of a very dark pit and stood me firm before my Father again, knowing that regardless of any sin, I am loved, valued, forgiven and free.

Having a right mindset is most important here, because this addiction, as with all other addictions, actually changes the pattern of the brain and causes mental health issues. It is a hidden disease.

As the months went by, then a couple of years passed, I found myself entering into a season with God that I had only ever read about. It was like a personal revival and my relationship with Jesus entered into an intimacy I had never known before. His voice became so much clearer, His Word so much brighter, His presence would spontaneously bring me to tears and I felt a harshness and frustration begin to leave my heart and mind. It wasn't like the issue completely disappeared even during this time of heightened awareness of God, but it became less and less and I knew God was breathing on me and restoring me and healing me.

I dreamt I was with my old church friends and many of them were so angry (understandably), and due to their hurt were not able to forgive me fully. I started to walk home alone from this scene when loads of my old gangster and drug addict friends came to my side and took me into a nearby house. They showed me incredible support and grace. They loved me and encouraged me and could see I was wrestling with deep guilt issues. It was a very powerful dream and I woke up to the Lord's voice saying, 'Forgiveness! Some will, some won't, I have' and I knew I could no longer hope for and wait for certain people to forgive me. I had to now start to really live my life knowing that God had already forgiven me.

Forgiveness is such a powerful weapon and when we forgive others from the heart we actually set ourselves free, but we also empower people to press on and not be weighed down with their shame. In my experience I have found more love and support from unsaved and hardened men of the world than I have from many Christians! Not all, of course; God always has a beautiful bunch that offer undeserved mercy to the broken and hurting and sinful.

If that becomes our corporate attitude in this global epidemic called sex addiction (all addiction), then we will see so much fruit and many shipwrecked souls brought back to life and purpose. Come on, let's try this! It really does work.

Saturate your soul

I wanted to take a nice bubble bath earlier today. I reached for the bubble bath which was nearly empty but still had some liquid at the bottom. I tried to get it out by turning it upside down and even shaking it, but it was so thick it was clinging to the bottom and my efforts were in vain. Do you know what I had to do to ensure I could get it out and enjoy my bath? I just kept pouring in hot water from the tap until it poured out, and as more and more fresh water was poured in, the liquid could not remain. It was literally forced out by a more authoritative substance. As the water filled and refilled the bottle, it continued to force out the liquid at the bottom and the water became purer and purer. If we know Jesus, we are vessels of the Lord and although we are fully forgiven, fully saved and fully washed in the blood of Christ, we still need the ongoing and continual infilling of the Holy Spirit. Not a one-off experience, but a continual, daily encounter with the Lord.

Shame, especially, has a way of drawing us away from the infilling of the Holy Spirit, when being filled consistently with Him is the only way to walk in victory. Keep going after God no matter what and your life will soon be so full of Him there will be no room for anything else, but never ever become complacent and sit idly by, because the devil never does. It is only those who 'dwell' in the 'secret place' who 'abide' (NKJV) and so reap the many benefits listed thereafter in Psalm 91.

Psalm 91 is not the experience of nominal Christians or Christianity, but only the experience of those who 'abide'. Are you abiding? Or hiding away in shame? Living somewhere in no man's land? Make a choice now to saturate your life in Christ. I chose to get away from the TV and Facebook and any other distractions, and started spending at least two hours a night just watching documentaries and videos on revival, reading books, Scripture, and praying.

I became consumed with an appetite for God's presence until all else paled in comparison compared to knowing Him. *Fill your life with Jesus, flood your soul with His Word and refuse to quit even if you stumble or fall. Keep filling, being saturated and overwhelmed with the goodness of God.*

Every day without intention we receive some 'liquid' into our vessels. It might be a few repeat glances at a pretty girl walking by, or a simple advert or raunchy dance routine on TV; a sexualised dream that was outside of your control. It can be old memories from past encounters and you may not be aware that it's been sitting in you until it's too late. Rather than fighting to remove this as I did for a decade, better to just create a routine of devotion and discipline where you spend regular and intentional time with the Lord and fill yourself so full of Him in that encounter that any hidden agenda of your flesh to yield to sin rises to the surface and is poured out in prayer and worship. *Get it out by getting God in!*

Lay your life down afresh for a daily commitment to spend time alone with the Lord. It is absolutely vital if you are to overcome temptation, know your God and live a powerful life in Christ.

I was just praying for this book and what God wanted to say next and as I lay with my eyes closed, listening and waiting, I saw a group of mountaineers climbing along the sharp face of a cliff edge. The guy upfront, the pioneer, was carefully going ahead and they were all connected together by strong links and tied into one another. The pioneer came to a narrower footing and slipped and fell. It was a very high cliff edge and would have meant certain death if he had not been tied into the others in that group who were still standing on sure footing and could now see the danger that their pioneer had not been able to see.

What stopped this man falling to a horrible death was the team spirit, being connected and their corporate effort to pull him back up. If they had cut the connection, this helpless man would have surely died. I feel what the Lord is saying is obvious: that the Church requires pioneers; God calls some to go ahead and lead the way, and we must ensure they are safely connected to the rest of the body and not just cut them off if and when they stumble, or slip.

The body must protect each other and offer support. We must stand together in this battle and we must remain diligent to stay committed to each other. A team spirit and family spirit will surely empower us like nothing else can. Stay connected and stay part of a community. Do not walk alone because there will be no one to help you when you fall (see Ecclesiastes 4:10; Hebrews 10:25).

If you have found yourself walking alone or you feel rejected and isolated, remember it is still God's plan for you to walk in relationship with other believers and stay accountable. Do not be like Elijah in 1 Kings 19:10 and think there is no one else left when there always is.

Let me tell you a dream I had regarding a well-known evangelist. In the dream I was with my wife at a church and we were sitting in the second row. The pastor was on the platform and was very graciously trying to introduce him as the speaker and he was saying to his congregation that despite falling and hurting the Church, God was trying to restore him back to ministry and wanted the people to receive him and the gift of God that was still operating in his life. The congregation became very agitated and many were booing and shouting out accusations and condemning him. He tried to get up and preach, but the more he did the more aggressive the congregation became, until he finally gave up and sat back down on the seat next to me and looked very broken.

I began to sob and sob as I asked him to forgive me for judging him. The congregation continued to boo and shout abuse until Lydia had had enough, and she stood up and shouted these words: 'Why don't you all stop judging him, and just start loving him?' She sat back down. I woke up and again I believe the prophetic word here is very clear: the Father is seeking to restore many fallen and discredited soul winners and leaders back into ministry and fruitfulness, and He wants us as His Church to receive them when they are welcomed back by the pastors and others who are willing to take a risk and use them again.

I believe under the inspiration of the Holy Spirit that it is time to love the wounded back to life and see them (as many as possible) restored back to their God-given purpose and flow in their grace and anointing.

Pray:

Lord, help me to be one that You can use to love the wounded back to life from both sides of this issue. Help me to see with Your eyes and feel with Your heart.

Chapter 10: Valley of Dry Bones

In Ezekiel 37 we read about an incredible encounter the prophet Ezekiel has with the Lord, and how he is taken by the Spirit to a valley filled with dry bones and has this incredible encounter with God concerning this terrible sight. Ezekiel reveals to us all a huge characteristic of God's nature and passion. In fact, it is this insight to the core of His character that gives me so much passion and purpose. God always wants to breathe life into seemingly dead situations. He loves to resurrect, restore and create.

The reason I turned to this chapter in Ezekiel is because one night as I was drifting to sleep I heard the Lord say to me, 'Breathe on these slain, two verses before', that's exactly what I believe He said to me. I knew the verse was familiar so googled it and turned to Ezekiel 37:9 and then excitedly looked at verse 7, wondering why God was trying to communicate to me in this way. I love that God is so relational and even at times says and does things that mean you have to look deeper and draw closer to understand. He loves to woo us into a more intimate relationship with Himself.

In chapter 37:7 Ezekiel says: 'So I prophesied as I was commanded ... And ... there was a noise ... and the bones came together' (NIV). I knew that God was speaking to me.

1. He wants me to prophesy unashamedly as I have been commanded.

2. He wants me to speak out about this subject now (releasing a sound).

3. He wants us to come together on this issue and face it head-on as one body.

We must all come together on this issue!

Because Jesus is a life giver (see John 10:10) He wants to take your seemingly lifeless situation and your hopeless circumstances and turn them around so that there is now incredible life and passion again. That is the mark of true revival.

God is a revivalist at all times and seeks to bring life, purpose, blessing and joy, turning situations around and creating glorious testimonies that move the heart of others to see His glory. His nature is as a life-giver, a deliverer, a healer, a restorer. *He is not intimidated by really gross or desperately dark situations. He can bring life and transformation to absolutely anything and anyone.*

The Hebrew word 'dry' originates from the word 'yabesh' which means to be ashamed, confused or disappointed (as failing) or withered away. To be all dried up. I knew when I saw this after hearing His voice that God was not only breathing on the slain but He was also breathing on this book.

I was finding it so difficult to find the time to write it and it sat for weeks with just an introduction and outline for a few chapters and some notes and some thoughts. I felt God prompt me to get going, but life kept getting busier and I kept making excuses to delay. I was escorting Lydia to an event in Windsor where she was co-leading worship; one of the main guys who helps lead the church and much of the ministry is a guy called Tomi. I had never met him before, nor did we speak other than a brief 'hi' and 'bye' in the green room. But then Tomi made a beeline for me during one of the breaks. I was sitting with Lydia and my son Callum. We were eating and waiting for the next session to start when Tomi came and joined us and wanted to minister to me. He began to prophesy, and of the hundreds of prophesies I have received over the years this was the most detailed and accurate word I had ever had.

It was breathtaking and my wife and I both wept as he called me out and revealed my heart, dreams and visions God had spoken to me many times but very few knew about. Part of the prophecy went like this: 'The Lord says that in this season it is time for you to put pen to paper and finish off the half-finished books and half-finished projects.' (I had two half-finished books and several projects sitting on my computer!) He said: 'God is going to open this book up to the world in a unique and dangerous way and I am seeing some of the pages and it has to do with testimony, and bondage and the hand of the Lord to deliver.' I was a mess at this point because I had known this book was of the Lord, but several times shame held me back from writing; this prophecy released me from that and I have been writing furiously ever since. He also said: 'Some big names will rise up to try and black ball you but the Lord declares His new righteous standard over your life … they didn't make you and so they cannot break you.'

I wasn't so much in a dead, dry valley situation any more at this stage but it certainly breathed life on anything that was still slain within me, and added some flesh to all that God had been graciously doing over the last few years.

Part of the prophecy included: 'In the past you were a man who knew what it means to self-medicate and know what addiction is, and what God did in you He will do through you in a moment' and within a very short time I had seen one of old friends who was heavily addicted to drugs and gambling set free. He is now walking with the Lord, literally overnight.

I was preaching in Northumberland in the UK and a man came to me who had been heavily addicted to heroin for twenty years and was still heavily medicated with methadone. After repenting and giving his life to Christ he was delivered and set free, and is still free today without any of the side-effects that it is humanly impossible to avoid.

God is stirring me daily to seek Him and His power to deliver the addicted, and He is raising up a people filled with Himself who know how to deliver the oppressed. Maybe you are not addicted but have a passion to see others set free and be used by God in a powerful way? I encourage you to get the revelations inside of you and pass them on to those you may be leading, or your co-workers, and become a part of the army of people God is raising up to deliver this generation and warn the next.

One of the prophetic words I feel God gave to me directly was: 'Wake up My Church to the crisis that is addiction' and if you believe that, then it is time to respond. Sex addictions must be giving 'prime time' and spoken about to the whole Church; we must wake up to the seriousness of it all and get busy setting hurting and addicted souls free.

As my friend in Northumberland said after getting his twenty-year heroin addiction broken by the power of God, 'Methadone is like liquid chains.' He recognised that he was a captive to this drug. Do we need to wake up to this, or what? Did Jesus not tell us in Luke 4:18 that He had come to set the captive free? To deliver the oppressed? And while we are often so busy arguing over theology and overly planning and discussing how to best reach the lost, surely we should be strapping up our boots and getting to it?

Only this morning I was in prayer and enjoying the presence of God when I started to drift off and I had a detailed vision. In the vision I was talking to a friend of mine and we were discussing a church leader we both know who is a good man. My friend was saying that he knew he was a good man but he was upset that he didn't open the door properly for another friend of ours and felt this church leader had his favourites. I was also defending this man and trying to reason with my friend about why he may have reacted this way. The whole time this was going on I was trying to put my army boots on because I had been called to go outside to the local community as there was a serious fire destroying the land and people were being killed. I knew it was serious, but the longer I was discussing 'insignificant' church issues with my friend I was losing the sense of urgency that I had previously been called to.

Suddenly it dawned upon me that I had better get outside and help the others who were committing to the rescue operation. I quickly strapped up my boots and headed outside, but I was only half-equipped and it was not because my church leader had not 'opened a door' for me or spent the appropriate amount of time training me, it was because I had been distracted.

I rushed to this field and noted how heavily the ground had been turned over and a great deal of digging had clearly been done while I had been sat inside the walls of the church debating church politics with my friend. I heard my dad (who passed away in 2000) shouting my name and I looked up surprised to see him fully dressed, ready for the rescue operation; a handful of others were also fully equipped but this made me realise that I was not. I was only half-ready and I had missed the meeting where everyone was charged with the task of putting out this fire and saving people from death.

Then I came round and sat upright and felt strongly the Lord wanted to say something so I began to write it all down and hear what I felt the Holy Spirit had to say.

You and I have been called to get out into the communities and rescue those who are perishing in the fires of hell, and we are supposed to be fully equipped to do so, but while we are busy debating over church issues and who said what and whether the pastor likes us or not, or if we have been giving enough opportunity or not, souls souls souls are in danger of perishing in the fire of hell.

Maybe your church leadership have recognised an unteachable or unsubmissive character in you? Maybe you are too busy debating the ins and outs of church politics and have become too complacent, apathetic or distracted from the Great Commission of Matthew 28 to 'make disciples'? Maybe it is time for you to lay down your life, strap up your gospel boots and head out into the field that has been richly blessed and turned over by the Holy Spirit in preparation for the people of God to go forth and save the lost? Maybe your pastor is human, and needs some grace from you, the same way you expect it from them! Maybe we could all repent for judging and backbiting and wasting time and being distracted and for being ill-equipped and missing the meetings where God has been trying to equip us? Maybe we have not honoured the evangelists whom God has sent our way over the last few years, and the church has played down the urgency of what is actually going on around us every day?

While the Church sleeps the fires of hell are threatening to consume our communities. Wake up today, go to your church leaders and tell them you want to be made ready for the battlefields and the valleys of dry bones and see many saved in your areas of influence.

If you are serious about saving the lost and feel ill-equipped maybe you should contact me via my website (see the back of this book). Reach out and we will be pleased to help empower you.

A couple of years ago when I was going through a particularly tough time in my mind concerning shame and regret, my son Callum, who is highly prophetic, told me that in the middle of the night God gave him a vision and it was for me. My ears always prick up when he speaks like that, due to the incredible accuracy of his prophetic dreams and visions. He was only ten at the time but his relationship with God was (and is) very real. He told me that he had seen me speaking at an old cinema. I was doing a series of talks based on being an overcomer. He named a few of the talks that I was doing, and the maturity of his vision and his delivery really touched me and filled with me fresh hope. God never ever wants any of us to be defeated or to stay broken. He calls us to overcome and prevail in His name, no matter how deep the wound or how dark the sin.

God used my ten-year-old son to empower me with hope, and I pray this book offers you something similar. Regardless of your age or whether you are in full-time ministry or not, God wants to use you to prophesy and to turn this land full of dry bones into an army of healed, whole and powerful sons and daughters of Almighty God.

You really can overcome, regardless of a million or more defeats in the past. It is in you to win.

I could go on and on about the countless prophetic words given to me over the last few years, but I don't have the space here to do so. God loves to call us out of darkness and dryness through the prophetic. His reaffirming word over our lives is a powerful weapon against all addiction and life-controlling issues. I absolutely love my relationship with the Holy Spirit, and without Him I know I would still be utterly bound by shame and therefore sin.

The Holy Spirit does not just 'convict the world' of sin (John 16:8, NKJV), He also loves to convict us (persuade us) of our righteousness in Christ, once we have turned to Jesus. If we know how righteous we are now through and in Jesus, then we are well on track to living a powerful, overcoming life.

What really excites me is how many churches and leaders I am hearing talk like this now. It is thrilling to see how the Church is maturing and waking up to truth. Jesus loves His Church and we must fight for its honour. The Church is beautiful when it is built on truth and love. I have spoken at many incredible churches and heard testimonies of the most amazing churches doing superb work. It will always be the hope of the world.

Pray this with me:

God, I want my life to count for all eternity and I want to be fully equipped and undistracted so You can use me most effectively. In Jesus' name.

Chapter 11: He Wants You Fully Yielded

The Lord does not want you to wait until you are perfect before you approach Him. If He did, then you would never come to Him at all. What He wants more than anything is for you to come just the way you are, but fully yielded.

I heard the Holy Spirit say to me 'He wants you fully yielded' one time, just before I was leaving to preach in the north-east of England. I preached this message and saw God move in a powerful way.

God does not want any of us to wait and He does not want any of His kids to have to try to get themselves all cleaned up and their behaviour all straightened out before they can approach Him. In fact, the only way to ever be straightened out and made whole is in His presence. 'In [His] presence is fullness of joy' (Psalm 16:11, NKJV).

When I preached this message, and told the church and the many addicted and broken people attending that night that they could come exactly as they were and God would receive them and work in them, if they only presented their lives, we witnessed a glorious miracle, including a drug addict of twenty years – mentioned previously – who came and knelt down right where I was preaching and felt he could finally come to God exactly as he was.

I wonder how many are in the churches today believing that to be fully yielded means to be completely dead to themselves and alive in God and living a perfect life? To be fully yielded just means to be fully presented before the Lord without any hidden areas or withholding anything from Him. *He wants you to present your addiction to Him, not hide in the shadows.* He wants you to present your anger, grief, fears, disappointments to Him, not pretend they do not exist. If you mess up, present it to Him; do not hide away in shame, even if it is a constant ongoing battle. Presenting it and yourself fully to the Lord is what He wants, and how you will get free.

I love getting alone with God now knowing I can do so without shame and I don't have to wait a few days, or go a few days without sin before I feel worthy enough to stand before Him. This way I get to spend more time in His presence and I feel more alive than ever before.

Everything the Lord does and says in your life is because He is passionate about you. He is passionate about being fully involved in all areas of your life and expects you to yield to Him if you are ever to experience wholeness and freedom. Everything Jesus achieved for you at the cross is realised during intimate times with Him in fellowship. So I am urging you to fully yield to the

Lord and give Him opportunity every single day to encounter your heart and transform your mind.

One night when I was in Africa, I noticed a mosquito on the floor. I grabbed my spray and gave it a blast and then finished it off nicely with the sole of my shoe. It was an effortless victory and I felt very proud of my attack against this insect. As I walked away, I felt the Lord say, 'How would you like to know how to walk in that kind of authority over sin and demons?' To which I immediately replied, 'Yes, please, Lord' because I have learned that if Jesus wants to teach me something, then I need to be fully attentive. I put some worship music on and began to pray and wait on the Lord until a scripture came to me and I turned to it. Then another and another and all of them had the same theme which was 'Get alone with Jesus!' and then He took me to the dreaded topic of fasting, but showed me clearly how *fasting is not about religious ritual, but about intimacy with the Lord.* Fasting causes the flesh to suffer and weakens its power, but it is not so we can be seen fasting or to afflict our bodies for a day or two; it is always about drawing closer to God in an intimate relationship.

Then our flesh is kept under subjection and our spirit man (our new self) is quickened and comes into alignment with the authority it has been given through faith in Christ. It was a very clear picture to me and I knew it was all about a lifestyle and not a momentary encounter. Many addicts and ex-addicts fall prey to the thinking that a one-off encounter with God (that quick fix mindset) will change everything. I implore you to believe for these kinds of encounters, as my life has been radically impacted by many of them over the years; however, walking in real authority over sin and Satan comes from a lifestyle of intimacy with God, not a moment. I am talking about having authority over the flesh (for which fasting is God's weapon of choice) and having a spirit man so quickened that you live out of it rather than wrestling constantly against the things you wish to avoid. Being quickened by God is when the Holy Spirit breathes life onto a portion of scripture or *He* opens your eyes to see something more clearly and fully. It is like the Lord Himself comes and validates what you are thinking or feeling. It is His manifest presence in that moment. Live in the Spirit and you will not fulfil the lusts of the flesh (see Galatians 5:16-18). This is not a seasonal thing, it is a lifestyle, and it is the life we have all been called to which sadly seems to be a dying trend these days.

I learned more clearly than ever before that only when we live a lifestyle (not a season) of intimacy and surrender to God can we develop the kind of faith that walks in victory over the world and the enemy around us. That's how Jesus lived, it's how He taught His disciples to live and it's how we must live today. As long as your heart is set to romance – that is, intimacy with God – and not ritual, you will encounter God in a very precious way and live in Him.

Romans 12 tells us to present ourselves as a living sacrifice, not as a perfect sacrifice (although we are certainly perfect in Christ, because of what He has done for us), and that is the way we are transformed. Not by hiding, but by yielding. Have you truly presented yourself to God? Offering Him all your strengths and weaknesses, gifts, abilities, past, present and future?

All of it belongs to Him if you are truly His. Give everything, give Him your porn addiction and the insecurity that is usually rooted in it, give Him your shame and regrets, give Him your fear of failure and your rejections and disappointment, and let Him be God there too. Let Him weave His way in and through it all until it looks more like Him and thinks more like Him and rises above it all, as He did at the cross.

If you need to stop reading for a while and just give yourself afresh to God and tell Him you cannot beat the addiction and you do not see yourself as He does, then do so. I am praying earnestly that you *come out gold* as a result of the Holy Spirit's investment in your life during the reading of this book and the days ahead. I know you are probably afraid of failure in case you let Him down again, because you have so many times before, but the throne room of grace is always open to you (see Hebrews 4:16) and it really is the only way to longevity of freedom.

I will share more later about the kind of attitude we must all adopt as we partner with God to see full victory. The reason we may not see fruit is because for all the quality revelations we may have about fighting and not quitting and fasting (I have written about these in a previous book), we need to come from a place of romance (intimacy with God). Instead, we often come from a place of ritual (religion) and fear of failing rather than faith in Him. For me, in the past my walk with God was driven but not faith-based, and I think this shows up in my previous writings! It was about becoming something, not about being someone.

Ephesians 2:10 tells us we are God's 'workmanship' (NKJV), and that he has prepared good works for us to carry out. I think this says we are all a work in progress. Yielding fully to God allows Him the constant opportunity to do His best work in our hearts.

I want to share a very exciting encounter I had with the voice of God some time ago concerning the shame I was still feeling. It was immediately after I had viewed some pornography and I shut the screen down and lay on my bed feeling dirty. I knew at this point that the worst thing I could do was to draw back from my relationship with God, and this encounter only fuels that conviction I have now that whenever any believer sins they simply must choose to immediately push forwards not backwards and allow the Lord to speak. I will share the conversation I had with the Holy Spirit with you as it happened as I feel it might help some of you a great deal.

Rob: Lord, I feel so dirty.

Holy Spirit: Therein lies the problem.

Rob: How do I stop?

Holy Spirit: *The absence of shame is the presence of Jesus.* Eight hours a day walking in the world and five minutes a day worshipping the Lord; who wins – flesh or spirit?

Then He gave me 1 Peter 2:11 which speaks about the war against our soul.

The Lord then began to show me things about my past, such as how my earthly father taught me to devalue women (I won't give details) but He said to me: 'If you grow up in defilement then defilement will grow up in you.'

I then waited on the Lord a few minutes and heard Him say 'Animal instinct' and when I questioned why, He said, 'Fornication is about survival to you.'

Rob: Explain?

Holy Spirit: Stimulant, coping mechanism, escapism, retreat. Pain and pleasure.

I heard these words and wrote them down and felt He was showing me that as a result of my pain growing up; I am well aware that others have pain from childhood but did not turn to drugs etc., but I did, and countless others did too, and the drug of choice became a way of escape. To most if not all addicts, it is a coping mechanism and a way of retreating from the pain itself, even if for a few minutes. Drugs stimulate the brain's pleasure sensors and that drowns out the pain sensors. All addicts are trying to escape something and so the Church, which has been anointed as Jesus was to 'heal the broken hearted' and to 'proclaim liberty to the captives' (Luke 4:18, NKJV) needs to come alongside the wounded souls so that we see the wholeness in others that we long for and that Christ died for.

I believe narcissism is at the heart of most sex addicts' behaviour and those egotistical outlets like porn and sexting. If a person growing up doesn't feel that greatness is in them from an early age, they'll begin to express 'need' for greatness. This is not only true of the people and leaders in churches addicted to porn but also the leaders, celebrities and everyday people out there and many others who hide behind their titles and positions and influence and receive the praise and accolade of human beings like a drug to their needy souls. I believe this all has the same root, but the devil knows all our weak areas and whereas one man might be addicted sexually, another man might preach and teach as if his church/denomination/group/business is elite. Insecurity is manifested in many different ways.

Rob: If You could say something to me that would change my life in a healthy/whole way, what would it be?

Holy Spirit: Goodnight, *son*!

As you can probably imagine that wasn't really the kind of reply I was expecting, but the Holy Spirit was incredible that night as He taught me about God, me and His heart.

Holy Spirit: I am all-knowing, all-seeing, and I still want fellowship with you as My son.

The Lord was showing me that even though I felt dirty and I had just been in sin, He still wanted fellowship with me, and this is a great anchor to me now and something I encourage all of you to get a grip of.

Holy Spirit: Apostolic greatness is in you. That's not what you really wanted to hear, is it, son?

Here I believe the Lord was showing me how many leaders try to encourage people by using grand prophecies – and these prophetic words may well be true. But the Holy Spirit was showing me that

He had moved me to a place where I was less concerned with the great prophecies and more concerned with having a deeper relationship with my heavenly Father.

Rob: No.

Holy Spirit: It is not about anointing sons, it is about affirming sons. You can never look for Me as hungrily as I look for you. I am interested in you, at all times. I have an unshaken interest in you and knowing this will disengage your need for sin. I am interested in your pain and the process, not just your progress.

This might sound random to some of you but it was a life-changing encounter for me. The Father is not just interested in how well you are doing and how many boxes you tick and steps forward you make. He is interested in your pain too and wants to lovingly heal it.

If Jesus was the One dealing with your addiction, He would not do so from behind a desk. He would do so intimately and lovingly and He would ask you questions (already knowing the answers) like He did with Adam and Eve when they hid in shame in Genesis 3.

Jesus would bring you to the root issue, not the manifestation of it because He deals with roots, not just branches. Jesus would leave you feeling like you were better than and felt more precious than gold, and you would feel less like sinning and more like the son or daughter that you are. He would not beat you up or put you down and He certainly would not label you evil or give you any other kind of shame-based title, He would empower you and set you free.

Did He shame Peter for violently attacking another man and cutting off his ear? Or for denying he even knew Jesus at all? How did Jesus respond? Look it up in John's Gospel – chapters 18 and 21. I am not saying He would overlook your sin, of course not, and yes, if you were 'religious' and hard-hearted He might rebuke you, but if He can see the brokenness in you and the desire for change, then He would ensure you came out as gold (see Job 23:10), not cast away like a broken pot.

The Lord showed me how I was raised with a 'get up and get over it' attitude and a 'man up' mentality (I cringe, knowing how zealously I used to preach this to people) thereby dismissing the very real need to have a loving Father kiss my tears away.

The gospel is all about wholeness not just abstaining from sin. If we live our lives focusing on resisting sin then we will have missed the purpose of the cross.

Pray:

God, help me to live daily in the wholeness and the joy of Your gospel. Help me to see the truth of Your good news and live aware of it, regardless of what life brings.

Chapter 12: The Journey

There is a very clear principle in the kingdom of God and it is definitely applied very diligently to all addicts before they come to Christ. It is vital it is applied even more passionately when it comes to pursuing God and ongoing freedom. It is the principle of persistence. *All addicts are wired to want and even need a quick fix.* The brain says 'I want it now' but the addict will also be incredibly persistent in getting it 'now'. The addict wants it immediately, but certainly does not give up easily in their effort to obtain their drug of choice. In fact to many addicts, a great measure of the thrill is within the pursuit of the high.

It really is irrational if thought about logically that a man like me would have spent hours, even days, pursuing the money to buy a £10 crack stone knowing that it would only last a matter of minutes as a high before the need for more would kick in more strongly than ever before, and again the hunt for cash or drug began. It is absolutely absurd when you look at it rationally, but as any drug expert or therapist will tell you, the part of the brain used for pleasure also bypasses the reasoning part of the brain and so an addict actually is not in their 'right mind' during the hunt for cash or drug of choice.

I used to go to incredible lengths to beg, steal or borrow cash when I was addicted to crack cocaine. I would invent all manner of stories and be extremely convincing because I was so desperate and my brain needed another hit. It had been hardwired through repeat use to need this fix and it would not rest easily without it.

Sex addicts certainly do need to put principles and protection in place during 'sane moments' to protect them during the process of their freedom. For example, definitely get a strong internet accountability programme on all your devices so that in weak and vulnerable moments your 'go to' has been removed. Make it as difficult as possible to feed your addiction. I know only too well that during a moment of weakness and 'need', the last thing you will do is the very thing that you should do and that is ring your pastor or accountability friend. Pastors/friends, if and when they do ring, *please* do not just tell them to go to the cross; this only highlights our ignorance when dealing with this issue. If you have never been addicted yourself, you most likely will never understand how it works and so you might struggle more than an ex-addict would with judgement and harsh discipline. Guard yourself from that and get equipped as best you can so as to more effectively help someone else.

If you are addicted, when you are not in that heightened state of need for pleasure, do be courageous and pick up the phone and invite someone else in to help you. Same sex, of course. Although you cannot avoid walking past every pub if you struggle with alcohol abuse, or avoid every shop that sells porn mags, you can at least do what you can to 'cut it off' as the Bible teaches in

Matthew 5 and limit or 'damage control' while the Lord is doing the deeper work in your life.

I had to totally remove myself from familiar places and faces when coming away from the cocaine world I was so deeply involved in. I had to move towns to avoid the temptations and risk of failure to abstain. However, now I can walk past any of those old places and I actually meet up with some of the old faces and I am free of those temptations. I have a grounding in that area that means the boundaries can be extended. I now reach them and influence many of them, not the other way around.

For a time you may have to do something radical if you are serious about freedom. I moved four hours north and left my only son at the time to get my freedom. I had to seek God and there were was a great price to be made initially, but the reward was far greater and I have no regret at all about those decisions in the early days. I still have a very strong accountability programme on my phone and my laptop. I am under no illusion that where I am at right now in my journey, that decision to set up accountability is probably the reason why I never once looked at porn during my latest trip to Africa, staying in a room by myself. I am hoping and believing that eventually, like with the cocaine addiction in the past, I will be able to extend the boundaries and have more freedom. Right now you just might need a time of increased accountability and more limited access to the internet or even some people.

My attitude to the ongoing freedom from addiction really is 'whatever it takes' because it is driven by a 'I want more of You, Lord'. I guess the real question is: how badly do you want freedom and how hungry are you for His intimate presence in your life? It's not that you earn more of Him, it's just that you become aware of more of Him in your life, and that is the healing, freeing, empowering presence of Jesus to your weary, hurting soul.

You can delete or block any phone numbers that you might usually go to for some sexting pleasure. I know only too well that you can soon develop another number or two but at the very least, to honour God we must do what we can, naturally, to avoid temptation and sin. Cut it off as best you can, even if that involves some radical decisions, because although this alone will never get you free (not sustainably), it will draw the attention of God when He sees it is being done in faith and in sincerity of heart.

To think that the entire responsibility for our freedom rests solely on God is absurd. Yes, He is the only one who can root out and heal the deeper issues, but we are co-workers with Christ and definitely need to faithfully do all we can while depending on Him alone for the miracles, healing and deliverance.

'He is a rewarder of those who diligently seek Him' (Hebrews 11:6, NKJV). Ex-addicts and those still addicted need to lose the quick fix mentality ASAP when it comes to their lasting freedom. Of course believe for a miracle, and I can give many testimonies of those, but as I learned the hard way, after the miracle we must understand the principle of persistence. We must learn the ongoing journey/lifestyle if we are to sustain freedom and move on to effectively rescue others.

I definitely had a miracle touch from God that delivered me practically overnight from a deep-set and gross addiction to crack cocaine and even the porn too, but I became complacent and let porn back in. It came back with a vengeance and I suffered deeply, as did others around me. I encourage you to pause now and read Luke 11:24-26.

I am deeply concerned, as you may have already figured out by much of the Church's lack of understanding concerning addiction. The Lord spoke very clearly to me during the night some time ago saying: 'I want you to wake up My Church to the crisis that is addiction.'

The word 'journey' means to travel from one place to another, a passage or progress from one stage to another. We are all on a journey. Of course if any believer is not making progress in their personal faith and freedom, then there must be a problem that needs immediate attention. However, quite often you cannot see the progress yourself and need others to encourage. On the flip side of that, we are often too quick to judge someone else's journey because they are still doing something we are not, or they do not have the same level of faith as we do in a certain area.

In Numbers 33 we read about the Israelites and a portion of their journey; how they moved from Rameses, which was a place of slavery/bondage, and how they journeyed to a place called Succoth, which basically means 'temporary shelter'. People often start off bold and excited to leave their slavery, but then they seem to settle in a temporary place and do not make the rest of the journey. I want you to see some 'prophetic types' here – that is, how there is a clear picture mapped out for us hidden within the names, and the meaning of the names, of some of the places along the Israelites' way.

From slavery they moved to a temporary place and sadly so many stop there. They fail to recognise that God has so much more for them, and if they would only press on they would discover such a thrilling life in Him that many fail to find. Succoth represents the place where a decision to get out of slavery has been made, but as things still seem tough and there seems little benefit or little opportunity for real change, we choose to give up and return to our former ways.

I have seen countless people make this grave mistake because they just didn't find that deeper resolve to press on in faith. Due to either a false gospel being presented to us or a failure to understand how the 'narrow' road of Matthew 7:13 is, at times, extremely difficult terrain, we quit the journey and slide straight on back to slavery. The cares of life and the hardships around us seem too much and so we quit. Please do not be such a person as we find in Hebrews 10:39. Ask the Lord now to put some guts in you and some tenacity in you, and move from the temporary place and onto the greater and deeper things in God.

Etham was the next stopping place for the Israelites. It was near the Red Sea. As many of you will know, the Red Sea was the place of incredible breakthrough, deliverance and miracle of God – read Exodus 14. But time and time again while on the boundary of breakthrough, so many turn and flee, believing the journey too difficult. They find themselves settling in a temporary place. Not necessarily returning to slavery, but yet still not breaking through.

I was one of these people, and I would look ahead and wonder if there was anything more, anything greater, anything more liberating, but I allowed certain people and certain things to hold me back. We must learn to really overcome the fear of man and the fear of the unknown and trust God with our lives. He really can be trusted fully.

I could go tirelessly through all the places the Israelites travelled, and the meaning of their names, and find something clever to say, but I just want to make the point that we are all on a journey and some are further ahead than others. We must learn what it means to press on. Matthew 7:8 says we need to keep knocking and seeking. Keep believing and trusting, and wherever you are on your own road with God, discover what your new life is and means. *It is the most precious new life and your life is most precious.*

As you figure stuff out and navigate, experience, wrestle and toil and win battles and lose others, the Red Sea is ahead. The Lord has already parted it and the way through is freely available to you if you just keep moving on in faith and trust your heavenly Father.

After escaping the Egyptians through the miraculous parting of the Red Sea, the Israelites eventually entered a place called Sin which means 'thorn'. What? We break through in a miraculous way and still find there are rocky paths and thorny bushes ahead? News flash! Being a follower of Jesus is not easy. Paul the apostle in 2 Corinthians 12:7 speaks of a thorn in his flesh (a human weakness) and although the Bible doesn't tell us what it was, we can see that Paul was an ordinary man with frailty and weakness like the rest of us. Despite his great stature in life and ministry, and his incredible influence, the Lord saw fit to make mention of his problem.

This should encourage us all on our journey that every single one of us has an area of vulnerability and needs the grace of the Lord. Numbers 33:12 says: 'They journeyed from the Wilderness of Sin and camped at Dophkah' (NKJV). Dophkah means 'knocking'. The people of God must continue to journey on, press on and push forwards. We must trust Him that when we do so He will meet us. He is never at rest when it comes to dealing with His pride and joy, which is you and your heart. A constant knocking as Jesus clearly taught us in Matthew 7 as a kingdom principle will attract the attention of God, and the Holy Spirit really will open the right doors at the right time. The Bible teaches us clearly that we must 'endure unto the end' (Matthew 24:13, KJV) and how there is a great reward for those who refuse to quit and lay down and die in the dirt of life. Keep knocking and seeking and trusting and believing, because real faith is proven by such qualities in the darkest of days and the wilderness of life.

We must continue to draw closer to God even if we are carrying burdens, shame, habit or addiction, and this kingdom principle will begin to champion our cause and see us through into a glorious breakthrough. Do not lose sight of this principle and expect everything to become all fluffy and nice and a sweet bed of roses immediately after becoming a Christian, because that simply is not reality!

Jesus Himself clearly knew about the journey of life and He Himself is our perfect model. He knew when to walk and when to rest, when to react and when to remain, when to do and when to just be. He knew all this because He was continuously intimate with His heavenly Father as you and I must also be. *Without intimacy we are absolutely defeated in the unseen spiritual realm and therefore crushed in life.*

In Numbers 33:13 we read how the Israelites moved from a place meaning 'to knock' to a place called Alush meaning 'to knead bread'. I urge you as one struggling with addiction or one simply looking to know more about the Lord to continually knead the bread of life, which is Jesus Christ. Seek Him, hunger for Him, live only for Him, work your life full into His by way of kneading – pressing, folding, stretching.

Jesus Christ really is the bread of life (see John 6:35) and so many so-called disciples fell away when it came to the teaching of Jesus found in this very challenging chapter. Oh, how I have learned the indescribable pleasure of kneading the bread of life. Yes, I need Him, and so I knead Him! I press into Him, I work all of my life into Him and who He is, and I urge you all to do the same. I have never known a season like the one I am in right now and my eyes are filled with tears as I smile in His presence at how He has and is and will continue to bring me through into fullness.

Knead away, knead and knead and knead, and only then will you see the 'need' for any form of drug pale in comparison to needing more of Him, because your mind and your heart and your entire being has been kneaded into the bread of life. As He becomes your all in all, you will lose your need for drugs and lose your need for the affirmation of people. This will happen when you discover the secret of kneading the bread of life. When you move to a place called Alush you will soon see how *A lush* relationship with Jesus is the very reason you were born! Enjoy Him every day and saturate and permeate your entire life in the One 'who is, who was, and who is to come' (Revelation 1:8).

If you know the Bible and the story of Joshua and Canaan, which was a place of incredible fruitfulness, conquering and victory, then I hope now you are stirred in your spirit to press on. (If you don't know this story, read it in Numbers 13-14.) Get up and get going and let the Lord deal with you as you journey and trust Him at all times. I am not saying I am fully 'in Canaan' now but I am definitely saying I am no longer in Rameses, that place of slavery, and I am so much further ahead than I was.

I have faith, excitement and passion right now as I know there is a whole lot more of God to enjoy and land to conquer. Thanks to Jesus, by faith we can move from slavery to victory in one moment, yet in the natural realm here on earth we spend a lifetime working that out and realising exactly what He has done for us on the cross and through His resurrection.

In John chapter 4 Jesus was on a journey and in verse 6 we can see that even Jesus Himself was at times wearied from His travels. Life can really suck us dry at times; sometimes it seems like we have nothing left to give or lean on, but God cares and God comforts and God loves us. He gave rest to Jesus and a reprieve from the oppression of the devil and He will do the same for you. Jesus is our model and we can learn more from Him than anyone else. Study the life of Jesus, get serious with your relationship with

God and devour the Gospels and good teaching on the cross and the Christ. If Jesus was weary, then why should we expect to be any the less? Jesus was not alone yet still He was tired, He was human and He was tempted and He was vulnerable and He had nothing but full trust in His Father to see Him through. For the temptations He faced, read Matthew 4.

Acts 1:11 says Jesus will return to this earth the same way He left and Luke 18:8 tells us clearly He will be looking for faith. Not big shots, superstars or megachurches, but faith – real, honest, vulnerable at times, often full of questions, but faith nonetheless, and the kind that refuses to quit and settle back in sin. Faith that overcomes is only found in the secret place relationship with the Holy Spirit, not by sitting on a warm comfy church seat for a couple of services each week. *Real faith, genuine intimacy, is forged in adversity and adoration.* There is no other way and so we must settle this now or we have no hope of being all God believes we can be through Jesus Christ.

Like Jesus and the lessons found in His life, we must get to the well, drink from the well of salvation and draw from the life flow of the supernatural spirit of Almighty God. You are a friend of the bridegroom (see Luke 5:34) and you are a child of the King, and with or without addiction, He delights in you. Knowing this will set your heart ablaze and your life on course.

At this well Jesus met a broken woman who we can learn from her history had a very clear problem. It seems she could not settle with the same man; she was either always hungry for more or she was repeatedly rejected due to some other issue in her life.

But Jesus dealt tenderly with her and restored her to Himself. He restored her to her God-given calling as a powerful evangelist and soul winner. It seems to me she learned what it is to move from endless lust to eternal life.

Get back to the well and abide there. From the well flows ministry and gifting and purpose, but Jesus made it clear that it must operate out of true worship which comes from the spirit and the truth – see John 4:23. A woman who had five husbands and another man on the go clearly had issues. Can you imagine such a woman in our modern world? Perhaps she would have been on Tinder, sexting and watching porn? Sleeping around and enjoying her gross sin? Yes, she was a broken, insecure, addicted woman who met Jesus at the well and became a powerful woman of God. She was already powerful, it just took Jesus and true revelation of worship to release her into her destiny. It is the same for us all.

I agree with the leaders who preach that true repentance should mean we give up the sin completely; I just understand that there is often a process and a journey, and the length of time between Rameses (slavery) and Canaan (fruitfulness) is determined by how quickly we can meet Jesus at the well of salvation and true worship. It is also determined by how diligently we fight to remain at the well and not get enticed away by opportunity and the entrapments of the enemy who is jealous because he is forever forbidden from the well.

The greatest lesson we can learn from John 4 and the woman at the well is worship. I wonder often if worship today is how Jesus intended it to be.

Jesus was at the well first, as a model to us all, and we must follow Him there and draw from that place. Jesus is the true well of salvation which springs forth with eternal life and we must re-establish true worship. Sunday morning congregational worship can be awesome, but a lifestyle of worship along the journey of life is where it is really at. I can assure you one of my main failures before any kind of moral failure was losing sight of true worship. It had become about the platform and Sunday meetings, everything was driven by Sunday service and building a perfect church which had the appearance of something great. Looking back I can easily see how empty it really was. I am referring to the values I was trying to establish. My heart was driven by what people thought about me, not by what Jesus had done for me.

Pray now that Jesus would meet you at the well of true worship, truth and intimacy. Devote some undistracted time right now or as soon as you can to simply enjoy His presence.

Chapter 13: Comfort My People

What an incredible chapter Isaiah 40 is as the great prophet of the Old Testament turns his prophetic anointing towards the Messiah who was to come and bring a message of comfort.

What is comfort? What was Isaiah hearing or seeing that so moved him to prophesy comfort and forgiveness to a nation he was so used to bringing judgement to? The word 'comfort' paints the picture of someone sighing out with pity and it shows us how the Father is a good God. He was concerned for His people and wanting to ease their suffering and He has never changed. God longs to relieve you of your suffering, pain, brokenness and addiction. He wants to bring you close to Himself and to His body, the Church, so as to remove your heavy burdens, shame, failures and regrets. He is concerned for you, cares for you, delights in you and wants to end your warfare.

This word in Hebrew for comfort also means to repent and this proves my point that God's preferred method of bringing us to repentance is not through heavy shepherding and harsh correction but through comfort and love.

Addicts seek comfort from their pain in the bottle, the needle, the pipe, the casino, the brothel, the internet porn, the countless apps that empower sexting and secret lifestyles, and it is mainly an escape from pain, not an arrogant attempt to con people and live a double life. It is an entrapment and a deception that they have been lured into, and before they know it they are in a filthy spider's web and completely powerless to get themselves free.

Have you seen that scene in the film *The Two Towers* in Tolkien's *The Lord of the Rings* trilogy, where Frodo is charged with the task of getting the ring back to the fires of Mount Doom? And how on his way he encounters a deadly and enormous spider that bites him, causes him to be completely paralysed, and then it wraps him up so tight in its webbing that he is utterly powerless to free himself? Then the very friend who Frodo had driven away because of his attitude and pride decides that he is going to remain loyal to Frodo even though he doesn't deserve it, and comes on the scene just in time to fight off and rescue the helpless Frodo from this giant spider, unravel him from the web and thus empowering him back on his mission?

What would the Church and the world really look like if instead of gossiping, judging and amputating the fallen Frodos (those who were really trying to fulfill their destiny) and instead chose as Jesus did to be loyal, valiant and fight for someone else's salvation, thereby empowering them back into the race? Frodo's best friend was Sam and Sam was uniquely loyal and brave and stood by Frodo when it would have been so much easier to turn his back, cut him off and walk away. That's what Frodo actually deserved, but like Jesus, Sam, the simple and loyal Hobbit ran to his friend's aid rather than from him. His love for Frodo and his sense of honour was far superior and so he rose up, headed into the bloody and messy battle and became the hero he was destined to be.

Jude 22:23 says we should 'show mercy to those whose faith is wavering' and rescue people (Jude 22-23, NLT); it tells us that 'love covers over a multitude of sins' (1 Peter 4:8, NIV); it tells us we should be careful not to judge lest the same judgement come upon us (see Matthew:1-3). We are all potential victims of the same sins so we should choose rather to fight for others rather than against them. Wisdom in Scripture tells us, though, that we must guard ourselves against the same sins so please apply practical safeguarding when addressing this sin, especially if it's your weak area (see Galatians 6:1).

Sam constantly offered Frodo *comfort* along the way, not because Frodo deserved it, but because Frodo needed it. Frodo had such good intentions and such a passion to fulfil his mission, but the mission was bigger than one man/hobbit and it required a friend! Are you such a friend?

Jesus ran into your battle scene and overcame the devil and He did so while you were His enemy (see Romans 5:8-10). That is a love and a version of Christianity that we must believe the Church can return to in this generation. That is a comfort so powerful that it has within it the power of God to restore the most broken, addicted and hardened man back to the Lord and back to His purpose on the earth. Jesus is the real Lord of the rings, He is the One who places the ring, not in the fires of doom, but on the sons of man who are called by His name and *He is the champion friend who always seeks to get you back on course no matter how risky, dangerous or messy your life is.*

Comfort means to ease the suffering, console, show compassion and be moved to pity. God chose to do all that to a nation that was far from repentant and had sinned so many times it's impossible to count; an entire nation that seemed hell-bent on witchcraft, rebellion, sexual perversion, violence and idolatry. Isaiah prophesied that the Almighty, holy, awesome God wanted to comfort them, wanted to ease their suffering and show compassion on them. Why? Well, simply put, because that is His nature.

You may be deeply entrapped in addictive behaviour and overrun with shame and guilt and feel paralysed and helpless, but there is a friend that believes in you and He does not run out on you, turn His back on you, speak negatively about you and He 'sticks closer than a brother' (Proverbs 18:24, NIV). Jesus is the model friend who clings to you. God will never leave you or forsake you, as we see promised in Hebrews 13:5, regardless of how desperate your situation is. Jesus is right there with nothing but good intention and the power to transform. He is working on your behalf.

When you have given your life to Jesus, you are not alone and you never will be. Jesus is by your side, the Holy Spirit is the One who comes alongside you and doesn't walk out on you when you act like a human being with weakness (even gross sin). He is the One who wants to get fully involved and walk you through the process and into the promise.

God so wanted Isaiah to be clear on the prophecy, and for the people He was devoted to to hear the word of the Lord concerning His heart towards them that He said 'Comfort' twice in Isaiah 40:1, which in Hebrew culture was literally like taking a yellow highlighter and running it right through the sentence, or putting it into big bold letters and underscoring it twice. He wanted to make a very important point.

God, your God, wants to comfort you not cut you off, heal you not harm you, pull you close not push you away, and He wants to show you compassion not confusion. Isaiah heard God say to speak comfort and be warm-hearted towards this desperately dark and rebellious people. What a sweet and encouraging Father we have in the Lord.

Perhaps a large portion of the Lord's people need to step out of the old covenant and the old wineskins Jesus spoke of in the Gospels and enter into His compassion and grace? *Holiness is not following rules, it is falling in love.* Fall in love with Jesus as He really is, a healer, deliverer, comforter, best friend, strong tower, mighty warrior, valiant Father, overcomer…

As you rediscover His good nature and His love for you, you will start to come away from the addiction and into adoration.

I believe you are escaping and the way back to the Father is not through isolation but through visitation. He wants to visit you with His presence and His passion for your heart and set you free and set you on fire.

The Lord prophesied through Isaiah in verse 2 of chapter 40 that 'her warfare was ended' and 'her iniquity [perversion, depravity, punishment, guilt] is pardoned' (NKJV) but still we feel that even if we can muster up enough grace to forgive someone or ourselves, they or we must suffer some punishment. When Jesus died on the cross He was punished for you and for me. *Jesus received the full wrath of a holy God so we could receive the full benefits of a loving God.* Read Psalm 103 and the benefits of the Lord concerning your life. Salvation, healing, forgiveness, rescue, wholeness. What kind of God is this? Your battle has been overcome by grace and your current experience has to come into alignment with the reality of heaven and your Father's word over your life.

I urge you not to read that I am saying sin is OK and we can live how we want; I am saying that if we discover this truth about grace, mercy, forgiveness and love then we will rather *view Him with eyes of love than view porn with eyes of lust.*

The fact that Isaiah goes on to prophesy about preparation and valleys being raised and mountains lowered and crooked ways being made straight only serves to emphasise that this comfort revelation should eventually produce right living, not loose living. I am a passionate advocate of holiness, regardless of my previous battle in this area. It has always been a deep-seated desire that drives me to believe for complete purity and to live the most sexually pure, consecrated, passionate, fully yielded life that is possible in Him. *The true comfort of the Lord must drive us supernaturally towards the consecration of the Lord.*

Remember, though, as this is very important, we are already holy (if Jesus is our Lord – see 1 Corinthians 1:30), fully loved, fully forgiven, fully accepted, chosen and valued. You cannot add to this or take away from it, except in your own mind. The Lord loves you deeply and that will never change. You are more valuable than you'll ever be able to reason or learn from any book (including this one). Only the ongoing, deepening relationship with the Lord through the Holy Spirit will set you free and keep you free.

I can honestly say I have never felt so shame free and as a result I have never known a time where I feel the temptation to view porn or cybersex so easy to ignore. It cannot be done through principles or rituals, or greater effort, but only through intimacy with Jesus. It's all about discovering your true identity in Him and the value He places on your life.

Pray for revelation of your true value to God.

Chapter 14: Perseverance – 'I Heard the Knock, Son'

Many live as though they do not believe what I am about to say, but God 'is a rewarder of those who diligently seek Him' (Hebrews 11:6, NKJV). He rewards hunger, diligence to seek Him out and draw deeply from His presence. He rewards good stewardship and He delights in offering Himself to those who follow Him more fervently.

I was waiting on the Lord a while back and heard the Him say, 'I heard the knock, son' and I knew He was referring to the way I had so zealously sought Him for victory over my sex addiction issue. The way I had tirelessly fasted and prayed (much of which was in the flesh, not faith) but there was over a decade of history between me and the Lord of ceaseless prayer and wrestling, and I had refused to quit until the battle was over. It may or may not always be in the background but my heart feels so full of God, my mind is renewed and seems to finally understand that sex is not my master and I do not have to give in to the cravings of my flesh.

This is more than just *knowing* what the Scriptures say, this absolutely must become experience. Are you knocking? Seeking?

Asking? Believing? Building a history with the Lord?

God opened my door and I entered into a relationship with Jesus that I had only ever read about. It is a supernatural intimacy that has given me an intimacy with the supernatural. I simply want Him so much more than any pleasure porn or a flirtatious conversation could offer me. That does not mean I am not tempted, but the closer I draw to Jesus the less authority the temptation has and now I realise I can never, and should never, and do not want to ever, go back to a walk with God that is not built on intimacy, vulnerability and transparency and grace-empowered holiness.

As John 8:36 asserts in many translations, I am FREE FREE FREE indeed because of the precious blood of Jesus and the out-working of the Holy Spirit who has so patiently and so passionately been bearing with me for so very long. He is becoming my very all in all and the breath I breathe is because He is the great I AM (see Exodus 3:14; John 8:58). He wants me to breathe, He wants me to live, He wants me to give my life fully in return for His sacrifice because that is His great reward.

How awesome it is that Jesus sees me and you as so precious and so valuable (despite all our weakness and mistakes) that He would choose us as His reward and the only return for His sacrifice that could bring Him true joy. The price that was paid that made incredibly good investment sense to the wisest, richest, kindest, most compassionate and caring, loving and giving Father. I can only repeat my new and lifelong catchphrase that 'You may have lost your way but you never lost your worth', not to a holy but merciful and loving God.

The Lord will fight for you when no one else will. He will war on your behalf and He will move heaven and earth to find you, free you and restore to you the true value and identity for which Jesus had to die.

Battle on in Him, not by yourself, but in Him and with Him. I am prophesying right now as I just saw a multitude (even a generation) of door knobs turning. I could tell the Lord was behind the doors and He was so excited and so joy-filled as He is finally getting to open the door to so many that have been knocking. I also see Him sitting behind other doors that are not being knocked on and the look on His face is of disappointment and great sadness.

He is disappointed that so many distractions are stopping you from knocking on the door that He so excitedly wants to open to you. A door of intimacy and victory because they must go hand in hand. Knock on, knock again, seek on, seek again, ask on, ask again, keep on keeping on. Dig in, press in, engage, refuse to quit or even slow down. Build yourself up for a more intimate life of prayer and worship and let God encounter you in supernatural ways.

We need a Christ-addicted generation to arise. Addiction is fuelled by the pleasure sensor of the brain being overloaded with a chemical that it cannot regulate naturally because the high is too quick and to strong. If we find a generation and empower them to *fix* their gaze on Jesus (see Hebrews 12:2), we will see a Christ-addicted generation overcome every other habit and compulsion that Satan has so ensnared this world with.

I am praying for such an overwhelming multitude of intimate

Jesus lovers to arise that the greatest invasion to our enemy's kingdom is seen and felt in this generation. I believe it will be an invasion of intimacy. Those who truly love the Lord with all their hearts.

My dear friends, Jesus is more exciting and more thrilling and more ecstasy-giving than any other high you can ever experience, and if He was not then I would have little or no hope to offer you, but He is. He is the thrill of my soul and with every encounter another wound is healed and another hole in my soul is filled.

Jesus desires to so satisfy you that the very thought of a drug, or porn, or an immoral sexual encounter literally pales in comparison compared to knowing Christ. The Holy Spirit must become so real to you that you know when He is pleased and when He is grieved, and when He is tugging on your heart so as to draw close. He will never let you down or leave you dry if you only learn how to truly abide.

Of all the creatures on the planet you and I are the only ones created for and permitted to walk with Him in the sweetest fellowship, friendship and service. The billions of other creatures merely display His glory, but you and I occupy His very being and He is jealous for you. 'Taste and see that the LORD is good' (Psalm 34:8). *Drink from the well of salvation, eat from the bread of life, dance with the darling of heaven and snuggle into the very heart of the Father.*

In that way your addictions will be broken because your heart will be filled and thrilled with the intimacy and the wholeness and holiness of the One who chose you, placed the value of His Son Jesus upon you, and gave up His very best so He could atone for your sins and restore you to Himself. Wow, Jesus!

He heard my persistent knocking and He opened to me. I did not come in without baggage, or without issue, but I came in and so did He, into the deeper places of my heart and He filled me and keeps filling me.

My sex addiction was not the problem, it was a lack of intimacy and abiding that permitted such a ruthless and unruly enemy to dominate and ensnare my soul. The keys to your prison are not in mere religion or in the appeasing of your soul with Christian works, but only in the presence, romance and thrill-seeking encounters with the very heart of Jesus Christ through the Holy Spirit. *The Father invites you in and the correction of your mind and behaviour is best worked out in romance not ritual, in relationship not rules, and in love not lust.*

You can pay all the money in the world and see every counsellor and therapist and expert there is, but if you do not discover the intimacy, romance and pursuit of God then you will never be truly free and you will never rise above your dictator and enemy, Satan, and the wiles of your old nature, and enjoy Him, Jesus, for all He is, and all He does and all He is yet to do.

If this book and the vulnerability of my testimony does not begin to press on that God-given and God created soul of yours so as to entice you into a deeper love affair with the Lord, then it has been poorly written. It becomes of little if any value to you at all.

However, if you feel the desire to worship Him and the intimacy of the Holy Spirit tugging at your heart, and if you respond fully and persistently, then you will be well on your way to ignoring the lusts of the flesh and growing in oneness with your Saviour, Jesus Christ.

Please just do not stop knocking on that door for He will most certainly reward you with Himself.

Pray:

Jesus, You silence my accusers, You heal my brokenness, You defend me even when I do not deserve it, You light up all the shadows within me and around me, and You still my stormy seas. You undo me, You see through me, You always knew me and You complete me. You are my safest place and my greatest friend. You are the rock on which I stand and the lover of my soul. I can never repay You or ever compare You, I can never earn You or try to deserve You, but I choose to receive You and love to enjoy You. You are the wonder of my soul, and the freedom I walk in, You are always with me and never against me. I cannot thank You enough but I'll live my life trying. I am forever Yours. You sing over me, and You are my eternal peace and prince of my heart. You satisfy me and constantly surprise me.

Chapter 15: Worship – the Doorway of Intimacy

Through the sacrifice of Jesus and the sending of Him by the Father, I am forever in debt to His love. I cannot pay back or offer anything else to Him that would be of right value, except love. I adore the One who died for me and gave His life in victory over my sin, shame and my ongoing need of grace and mercy. I am forever in debt and the only proper response is love. God did not send Jesus to die so I could pray more or study more, or do more, but so that I could be more. I could be His child and live for Him, my holy, awesome, indescribable Father in heaven. I pray more and I study more and I do more when I realise that I am more in Him than I can ever be elsewhere. My value to Him and in Him is infinite and priceless.

It cannot be paid for by anyone else or by anything else because the blood of Jesus Christ speaks of a better way (see Hebrews 12:24). I am now drawn into the throne room of grace because I know He is there. The mysterious yet revealed One, the One who was and is and always will be.

The power of the gospel demonstrated by signs and wonders and miracles is merely a greater invitation to walk through the doorway of intimacy and to be lost in the wonder that is Jesus. I in Him and He in me, my all in all and the One who completes me. Please read John 17:21-23 and pray the same prayer Jesus did in your own words.

God always seeks to draw our gaze away from meaningless pursuits and into the unending depths of His heart and nature. You will never find outside of Him what you can only find inside of Him.

Porn addiction or any form of addiction is primarily a result of not knowing Jesus intimately. I used to be so confused as a church pastor – how could I be three or four hours into prayer and Bible study and vision planning and yet still so easily fall into temptation? Now I know why. It was because I was so busy being a 'professional Christian' that I missed the purpose for why I am, which is to be with the great I AM in daily devotion and intimacy.

These days I prepare far less sermons (if any at all) and preach far greater ones, because I just speak now out of the overflow of my intimacy with the Lord. I was always a good orator but now I am seeing souls saved faster than I can count, bodies healed and miracles that are astounding me and others. Words of knowledge that are incredibly accurate and detailed and life-changing for those I am ministering to, because I have discovered the secret that so many before me have discovered. That secret is that the power flows out of His presence not our professionalism, or our pulpits, or our excellently presented platform ministries.

It is all flowing from the secret place of worship, intimacy and being fermented in His love, passion, purity and power through hearts that adore and drink deeply from who He is.

Make Him your all in all and He will always be more than enough for you.

To worship Him and to be with Him must be our great obsession. I can barely read Scripture these days without tears flowing from my eyes as I see Jesus on the pages and experience the closeness of His person within me and around me. I barely have time to even think about looking at porn, let alone wasting hours as I used to do viewing it and feeding from it, because a greater and deeper appetite has been awakened within me that mere religion, or the encounter of porn simply cannot compete with. To be with Jesus is to be, simply to be. He is my everything now and I value my time with Him so much more than I ever have because I know who I am in Him.

Outside of Him I am so confused and broken and carnal-minded. I draw near because I long to know Him just that little bit more every day. He is the reason I live and breathe. If ministry, or friends, or media, or career, even family, pull you away from knowing Jesus intimately then you must, absolutely must amend your ways and cleave to Him.

Worship is the greatest dimension of encountering God because we are exalting Him and drawing from Him and giving to Him what He alone deserves. The river that flows from Him and from His being (see Revelation 22) captures you and frees you all at once. You are drawn by His desire for you and it releases a desire in you for Him and nothing else. Miracles sit at the doorway of intimacy but miracles, signs and wonders are not the reward, they are merely an attraction towards the main attraction – which is Him. He is our 'exceedingly great reward' (Genesis 15:1, NKJV). He is the reward, not just the rewarder. Many seek God and praise God because they want or need a miracle, but the miracle is Jesus. The reward is Jesus. The fullness of the attraction and the signs and wonders point continually to Jesus as the ultimate sacrifice and reward for your soul.

As I have made clear in this book, the danger is when you have encountered God or made a conscious effort to worship Him and draw close and then still stumble or fall with your addiction or any form of sin, because the heightened state of your flesh coupled with the oppressor's voice and condemnation causes you to retreat and to think 'works-based' again. You must fall into deeper grace and deeper dependency.

This is the only way to go deeper and deeper until that unruly addictive pattern in your mind is so saturated and filled with the wonder of knowing Jesus that it starts to finally come under submission and you are ruling in Him, not in legalism or works. Then you must keep your mind and your heart constantly in a place of being filled. This is called abiding, or remaining; I have mentioned abiding above, but read John 15:1-10 to see what Jesus said about it. It is the most fruitful and powerful place you and I can ever live out of. We live out of His life flow, not our own, and draw our fruitfulness from the vine and the giver of life, and life 'more abundantly' (John 10:10, NKJV).

Worship is because Jesus is. Worship exists because Jesus does. We worship Him for who He is and what He has done and in faith for what He is still doing.

We cannot live powerful lives with a 'dip our toes into a religious experience' attitude. We need the fullness of who God is to be worked thoroughly and freely into our very being, and this does not happen outside of intimacy with Jesus. Through Jesus' work on the cross, dealing with the sin that caused our separation from God, paying the price for you and for me as a sacrifice for us – taking the penalty our sins deserve – we have been made righteous and can now stand before our holy King and enter His presence boldly, confidently, and find mercy and grace (see Hebrews 4:16).

I am saying this because we can never really worship Jesus unless we know who He is and what He has done for us. He did not just save us from hell, He saved us from ourselves as well, and He saved us to the gospel (see Romans 1:1).

Worship is not thirty to forty-five minutes of congregational songs being sung from the same song sheet week in, week out. That is not worship. I am burdened tonight as I imagine that a great proportion of God's people have only this experience in their Christian life. Worship is not having some well-known worship songs playing in the background as you talk with friends and occasionally glance at your social media sites. *Worship is where the oil of heaven is poured into your very soul because your soul is being poured out to God in adoration and humility.* I am sure that many Christians do appreciate this, but I have personally seen and spoken to many people who view their time of worship primarily as the few songs they sing before the preacher comes to preach. At the risk of sounding condescending, I am urging as many as I can to explore the deeper pleasure and freedom experienced when worship becomes an entire way of life, not just singing songs. Of course singing is absolutely a part/form of worship, but never let it stop there. Explore the deeper adoration of Christ that so many others have encountered and encouraged us to do the same.

We cannot say we are in worship when we have one hand raised and another on our mobile phones, or one eye on what God is doing and the other on everyone else in the room. Of course, it is certainly a good practice and has the ability to draw our gaze heavenwards, but real worship comes when you close the door and become unaware of anyone else but Jesus.

We can be the best Bible teacher in the world and still not live in adoration, and therefore for all our Bible knowledge and theology degrees we miss the power that flows from His presence and fills our very soul. You can have good experiences and enjoy church life and still miss Jesus.

Worship is the greatest form of warfare because it is where you and He meet as one and feed from each other in sweet intimacy.

I am not saying that you cannot have a deeply intimate encounter with God and then stumble in that same day, but I can assure you when you begin to live a daily life of intimacy and encounter with Jesus, and you become so hungry for Him that the promised infilling fills your very soul, over and over again, you will absolutely lose your appetite for drugs of any kind and sin of every kind and find a deeper desire to run fast after Him and into Him.

To attempt to find your victory outside of intimacy is merely idolatry, even when what you are trying and doing is godly in and of itself. Please take note of what I just said. If you remember nothing else from this book, remember that.

The devil's age-old tactic is to get us so busy (preferably doing his work, but he will settle for us doing God's work) that we have little or no time to just be with Jesus and pour out our adoration in Him. We preach, we evangelise, we sing songs, we cast vision, we have meeting after meeting and we still miss those moments that the Holy Spirit is trying to invite us into every single day so we become one with the Lord.

Jesus taught us that He and the Father are one (see John 10:30). We must learn what this means and how we can have the same level of intimacy Jesus had when He walked the same earth we are now.

You can soon fill your life with church and religious activity and still never know the thrill of one real moment in His intimate presence. We must not just fill our lives with God activity, but thrill our lives in God intimacy. Our adoration is the full measure of Christ's reward. By this I mean that Jesus' death on the cross and resurrection takes on full meaning only when we who have been redeemed offer up to Him a heart of adoration. Adoration is more than songs, it is more than good Christian practices, it is heart bursting daily with the deepest sense of love and intimacy. Adoration is a deeper, fuller, cherishing of His presence and devotion to all that Jesus is. My point being that so many of us can sing worship songs on a Sunday but so easily draw away from

Him on Monday when life gets busy. My desire here is to call you to a deeper, fuller and more meaningful relationship with Jesus. Give Him all of you, not just all that you do; only then will we give the world around us what it really cries out for, the living God.

Worship is the only way to even begin to walk in the holiness that Jesus is. Holiness is not something Jesus gives, it is what He is. He cannot give it to us aside from Himself, the way I can give my wife a gift that is not intricately connected to who I am. Holiness is Jesus. It is His person. We are fully holy through faith, not works; our faith is in Him and what He did for us on the cross. There He who 'did not know sin' became 'sin for us' (2 Corinthians 5:21); our being holy is because He is holy and He is in me and I am in Him.

I for one long to walk in that holiness every single day and to live such a pure life that just coming into contact with others they immediately sense there is something significantly different about me which points to Him, and draws them to His truth. I believe that true worship is the only way to produce true brokenness, which is the way to true holiness. By brokenness I mean to be undone by Him. To come to a place where to live just one moment outside of fellowship with Him is to know the greatest love sickness there ever was. To be deeply, intimately, consistently in love and awe of Him.

Jesus longs for our unbridled, unveiled worship. Let's live so laid down without restraint that we are utterly unconcerned with the opinion of other people and the persecutions or judgements, and we live fully His; where the deepest hunger in us is fed only by the deepest part of Him; where heaven and earth collides and it creates a seamless flow of intimacy with the lover of our souls.

Pray now that God would show you His deep desire for you to worship Him intimately and constantly through everyday emotions and life's ups and downs.

Chapter 16: Brokenness Produces Holiness

I think the simplest way of describing biblical brokenness would be 'a life poured out'.

We can see clearly in Scripture that God expects and deserves all those who profess to believe in Him and follow Him to do so fully, freely and without reserve. If I am to follow Him as Lord and Saviour, then it demands absolutes and no excuse. When Isaiah encountered the holiness of God in Isaiah 6 I can only imagine just how broken he was by his heavenly vision and encounter. I reel in awe at how this supernatural moment in his life changed him forever. Isaiah became in that moment a man obsessed with the call of God to impact the world around him. I have to question the authenticity of encounters people profess to have when it does not in some way at least move them towards a deeper hunger for His presence and His purpose on the earth, which is still 'to seek and to save the lost' (Luke 19:10, NIV).

The trouble with you and me is we do not submit easily and we have a million and one voices constantly surrounding us screaming 'live for yourself' or 'don't be so radical' or 'hold something back', but if you are ever going to be truly free and truly at peace in who you are and why you are, then you will definitely need to give everything you have entirely and without reserve to the Lord of your soul. It is how He made you to be, and anything less than everything will give Satan more opportunity to build misery in your life.

John the Baptist got it: 'I must decrease, He must increase' (see John 3:30).

John was the first prophet in Israel in 400 years and blazed onto the scene with incredible anointing. He was soon gathering huge crowds and stirring the nation of Israel in a very special way. He was radical, set apart, anointed, gifted, charismatic and fearless and could have so easily built himself up and drawn attention to himself had it not been for the fact that he knew he was born to lay his life down and serve Jesus Christ. John was filled from the womb with a deep sense of the call of God, yet still he freely poured his life back out as a gift to his Lord.

I want to suggest to you that *whatever you try to hold back from God will become a breeding ground for Satan.*

If a part of my life is held back from Him then it is idolatrous and poisonous and gives firm footing to the enemy of my soul to build an infrastructure of sin within me. I must die to myself (see Luke 9:23) and live only for Jesus because that is why I was made. God will not share His glory with another (see Isaiah 42:8) and He will not permit me to live half-heartedly and enjoy the full benefits of the cross and my new life in Him – although, of course, it's a journey!

In this chapter I want to urge you to discover the secret that all of the greats in God have. Pour your entire life out as a drink offering to the Lord (see Philippians 2:17) and live the fullest, freest, most passionate and powerful life you could ever dream of living. The more you give, the more you'll want to give, because you'll experience the blessing and the thrill of knowing Him intimately and as a friend. To give Jesus everything, including your pain, dirt, hurt and fears is to honour Him more than giving Him your perfect performance. He cares not for your perfect performance, He cares for the real you, to be fully bare before Him and completely at His mercy, because although perhaps we all doubt His trustworthiness at times, He alone knows just how faithful He is to those who try Him at the real faith level.

God expects holiness formed and fashioned out of brokenness while I believe the Church often expects holiness but only offers it from theory and discipline. The way to true holiness is to see Him in all His glory and beauty, grace and mercy, and realise that He still loves you despite how holy He is, and would still choose to delight Himself in you, a sinner – saved by grace.

In Genesis 7:11 God waited until the fountains of the deep were 'broken up' (KJV) before He opened the windows of heaven – the same way Jesus dying on the cross caused the earth and the veil in the temple[15] to be broken up, and the heavens opened soon after and released the Holy Spirit without limit. The same way

---

15 The tearing of the veil represented the way to God being torn down, Matthew 27:51.

that when you and I humble ourselves fully before God and our pride, rebellion, selfishness and our independence is broken up – then and only then can the true life flow of Jesus pour into our very soul and deliverance, healing, joy, passion and identity so fill our lives with Him.

The Holy Spirit cannot permeate a proud, arrogant, independent, rebellious, unteachable soul. *He must have brokenness before He can give holiness.* We cannot teach ourselves to be holy, we cannot discipline ourselves to be holy, we cannot beat ourselves into holiness; it must be a work of grace and impartation, and indwelling life found only in the Holy Spirit of Jesus.

The foundations of your deep must be broken up so heaven can pour in and through you. The fallow ground must be ploughed, the carnal mind must be conquered, the hurting heart must be comforted, the hard heart must be yielded and the rebellion broken before holiness can come. Holiness is not living a perfect life, it is living a broken one, in awe, in love, in grace and in adoration of Jesus.

We often think we do not have pride that requires breaking, but I assure you that very thought proves the foundations of your deep have not been conquered yet and so must be. Our resistance to the Word of God, the training and equipping of our leaders and those God sends to prophesy and stir us in the things of God, our constant grumbling and complaining, our apathy and our complacency are all signs that our deep, the deep place within our soul's foundation needs to be more broken before the Lord.

My God alone knows just how often I cried out for freedom from sexual addiction that was so rampant in my mind and in my flesh, but I had no idea I needed to be more broken. We think because we have cried a few times and offered up some form of confession or accountability that we are broken over our sin, but we are not; we must so crave the deeper things of God that it demands the very deep places within our soul to become poured out before Him in full dependency on Him. We must believe there is no sin too great to cause the love of our Father to shy away from us. It is His love and goodness that will break up what a million sermons never could.

Maybe you need to get before the Lord right now and ask Him with all sincerity to highlight to you any areas of resistance, and then cry out to Him to bring the foundations of your soul into a state of true brokenness so that He can have the whole of you.

Confession of sin, tears of pain and despair being offered to the Lord, the decision to allow someone else to hold you and love you in your weakest moment, bringing the real you, without mask and without agenda before God, will usher in His presence. He will give His angels charge to come to your aid and work a mighty work of grace in the very deep of who you are.

It is about collaboration with the Holy Spirit, not your own efforts and attempts that make you holy. Yes, we must partner with Him – but on our part we work at submitting, on His part He does all the deeper work that we could never do by ourselves. *We become powerful when we admit how powerless we actually are.* As I said earlier, if you could free yourself you would have by now.

One of the meanings from the Hebrew word for 'broken up' in Genesis 7:11 is 'hatch' and this is a great picture of what I am trying to teach here. We all go through so much as children growing up, and then as adults trying to be brave, and we feel like we must protect ourselves. We are fragile, like eggs; our soul is not made of iron as we like to believe, it is more like a fragile egg that we build great barriers and blockades around over time so as to protect just how fragile we really are. We dare not let someone else find out just how fragile we feel at that deeper level, in case they finish us off with a harsh word or a further rejection. God forbid anyone find out the real me... Isn't that true?

Well, someone must have permission to reach that fragile egg within you, and He will not force down your walls or your barricades, but He will patiently and lovingly enable you to let down your guard over time. I can assure you He alone can be trusted to break that egg and bring life from it, but I also understand how utterly difficult actually allowing Him to do so can be. You want it, but it will not come easy to anyone. Maybe it will be a brick at a time, over many years, but He is faithful, He is committed, He is skilful, He is undeterred and He is zealous to set you free by breaking up the deep foundations of your soul so as to get His heavenly flood to consume your life.

So many tragically settle for what I call a pseudo Christianity and church experience and merely dabble with a religious dose rather than enter into the fullness of His person and become one with Him through devotion.

He is not looking for your perfection, He is looking at you through His.

Another word from the meaning of 'broken up' in Hebrew is 'to break forth'. When God is allowed to break up the foundations of our deep He then begins to break forth with incredible intimacy, purpose and desire in us. We become as He always intended us to be, yielded and filled with Him.

It is your time to break forth with victory, praise and destiny, but the road ahead must be marked with brokenness or you'll never reach His goal for your life. To be broken up means to be divided – or separated.

We need a generation to break forth because they have been broken up. This is a mystery of the kingdom and ways of God, but it is time-tested and proven throughout history, and in those lives that have paid the price and offered Him the deeper places for Him to conquer.

I actually find it fascinating that the same word for 'broken up' in Hebrew is the word 'cleaving'. We must cleave to the Lord daily (regardless of how that day goes) and as the days, week, months and years go by, while constantly cleaving and trusting, and leaning in, He begins to break us up, shape our lives, and dig out the old foundations and set His new ones in place.

Our old, earthen vessel (our old nature; see 2 Corinthians 4:7, NKJV) must be crushed, broken up, struck by God, dealt a death blow and brought under, so as to break forth and experience the release of the Holy Spirit of God. Let me tell you that process is so much more than just speaking in tongues[16] and having some spiritual gifts activated. It is a far deeper place and a far more mature place to enter into.

In this passage of scripture found in 1 Kings 18, Elijah the great prophet of God hits the highlight of his ministry. Elijah was a man given to incredible miracles and powerful exploits and there was no one like him in his day, which is why we often refer to the 'spirit of Elijah' which is more than just a man, it is a movement; a people that carry the same fire and passion and breakthrough he did. However, he was also a man given to bouts of depression, insecurity and feelings of doubt. *No matter how great any man is, we are all so dependent on Jesus at all times.* In 1 Kings chapter 18 Elijah hits the bullseye of glory in what God is calling him to do, and brings about a stunning miracle and victory against all the false prophets of Baal, proving there is only one true, living God. There is so much to say on this victory, but I just want to make one main point here. After the victory, after the powerful demonstration of God and the throwing down of the false prophets, Elijah then calls all the people to himself and begins to repair the altar to the Lord that had been broken down (v. 30).

An altar in the Old Testament was the place of sacrifice and offering. In the New Testament (after Christ died and was resurrected), the physical altars no longer needed to exist. We become a living sacrifice (see Romans 12:1) or offering to Jesus, and carry about a

---

16 A gift of the Holy Spirit – a language we have never learned. See 1 Corinthians 12.

heart that is meant to be fully His, fully yielded and at His service. You could say the altar is our heart/soul/body/mind… Fully His!

My point is this: when God breaks something, or when God has intended to use something/someone, then He repairs it – or them. In other words, He does not leave you broken. It is a mystery, but God must break us to repair us and then He can use us for His glory. Being broken sounds terrible, it sounds painful, but it is actually beautiful, precious and incredibly powerful.

Once the Lord has managed to break us (through our submission, trusting, and humbling), He can then use us for His glory and we become who we were intended to be. This takes a lifetime and God does what He does in stages and with heavenly wisdom. He is so wise and such a glorious steward of our souls that He even uses all the pain, mistakes, past sins, present struggles, people, situations to aid His workmanship.

Nothing is ever wasted and no stone is left unturned. God loves to form us into who He always intended us to be before we fell so far from Him and lived for ourselves. He is the master repairer and the greatest shepherd of our souls (see 1 Peter 2:25). The word for 'repair' in this verse means 'to heal, make whole, healthy, to sew together, mend'…

This is glorious to me because I see that when God heals us from the brokenness of our lives He doesn't just heal us, He also makes us healthy; anyone can be healed in a moment under the mighty hand of God but it actually takes a lifestyle, not a miracle. Remember this: God doesn't just want you healed, He wants to train you and teach you how to live a heathy life (physically, emotionally, relationally, financially, spiritually) and although healing can be instantaneous, healthy demands intimacy and longevity. There is no quick fix here.

The Holy Spirit is restoring the altar of your soul as you journey daily with Him in Christ. Press on, be firm and aggressive in your pursuits of Jesus (aggressive in the spirit, not with people!).

You may feel broken, at the end of your tether and filled with shame, guilt and fear, but He is the repairer/restorer/healer/deliverer and He is focusing on you right now so as to bring not just healing but health and wholeness and victory. Trust Him and be like the clay in Isaiah 64:8 not the clay in Jeremiah 18!

God doesn't just want to break up your soul and repair your soul, He wants to break up cities and nations and turn them right back to Himself. He wants to use you to be a repairer of the breach (please read Isaiah 58), but God can only use us to the degree that He has us. Are you fully His? Or like the nation of Israel in Jeremiah 18:15 are you walking the 'pathways' (plural) or the 'highway' (singular)?[17]

We are called to a single highway, not many paths, and when we walk the pathways and not the highway we find ourselves lost, dead and buried in sin. When we take to the highway through faith we begin to live the life He always intended for us to enjoy.

Let God break you (humble you) and cause you to so trust Him

---

17 NKJV.

and want Him and need Him that you are soon willing to pour yourself out like a drink offering, as Paul the great apostle did. Brokenness is all about humility and the Lord's method for drawing out the real greatness in you, which is always Him in you.

Psalm 3:7 is such a powerful picture of what I am trying to say here. When God 'shatter[s] the teeth of the wicked' (NLT) it literally means He renders them powerless. We must become broken (powerless in our own abilities) to reap the immense benefits and blessings and purpose of His power working in us and through us. We must die to ourselves and live only for Jesus.

This kind of brokenness is like the great ship that sets sails on the vast ocean believing it can withstand anything, overcome anything (like the *Titanic*), but in all its own glory and power and ultimately pride. This great ship (our own power) could not see the iceberg up ahead and under the waters out of sight until it was too late. Human error/pride sunk the *Titanic*, not the iceberg, and until the great ship (your soul) is broken to pieces and finds itself at the mercy of the ocean of His grace, you will never find yourself where He planned for you to be.

The prophet Jonah, on his feeble attempt to escape from almighty God, found himself cast overboard and swallowed by the mighty fish and eventually spat out on solid ground within walking distance of his true destiny. That is a glorious yet terrifying picture of my point in this chapter and how only humility can bring us back to our destiny.

If you have hit a hidden iceberg and your soul is being flooded with the destructive waters of the world around you, then you can try to put your fingers in the holes and use whatever resources you have around you to stop the flood of waters filling you, drowning you, wiping you out of your destiny, but it'll soon be too late and you'll be a distant memory resting at the bottom of the ocean with no more hope for a future voyage. Unless you find what I call the 'bow of the ship', with all your life and its stuff behind you, and bow your knee to Jesus in full, humble, surrender. Do it now, confess your issue, come out of the secret closet of sin and come out gold!

Jonah 1:4 tells us about a ship that was about to be broken and utterly destroyed with all the cargo and crew and passengers on board unless Jonah humbled himself and came back to his destiny moment. Get off the boat now, the boat of pride, self-belief; the 'I can do this' attitude is killing your soul faster than porn ever could, faster than any drug could. This book is speaking to two groups of people – those who need help and those who need to be the help!

In my pride and also my fear of rejection I nearly took a ship full of people with me to the spiritual grave instead of jumping overboard and crying out for real help. Jonah only needed three days in humility before God repositioned him at the entrance of his destiny. People may ask you to take a year out, but God could do it all in less than a week if he finds you humble and ready to trust Him and the currents and waves of His love and grace. Sometimes God's love looks like the inside of a great fish, or if your sin is illegal, not just immoral, it may look like the inside of a prison cell, but whatever it takes, get off this boat called pride and escapism and throw yourself at the mercy of a heavenly and loving Father. Your true destiny is waiting for you.

In Ephesians 2:14 we can see that Christ has broken down the wall that separated and divided us from God and stood like a mighty smoke screen so that we would not see the truth. Our pride built this wall and only His blood, His sacrifice on the cross, demonstrating His limitless love and insatiable hunger to have us home again, could tear it back down. Make sure the wall is really down, that you can really see Jesus and the Father who delights in you, and do whatever it takes to keep this wall down.

Do not let religion, politics, fear of man, fear of rejection, anything or anyone, build this wall back up. Come through the broken wall into the throne room of grace and humble yourself, laying your entire life before Him, and stay there, forever humbled, broken and contrite and fully His.

The woman who poured out her broken life in Luke 7 knew what it meant to be beautifully broken, forever humbled and in awe of His love and goodness. I encourage you to read this story now and ask the Holy Spirit to speak to you personally and open up this passage to you in a personal and powerful way. He will because He loves you!

Let's go!

Contact Details

To follow Rob Joy and his ministry, or to otherwise contact him:

- kingdomcause.community

- therealrobjoy on Facebook

- Robert Joy on Facebook

- RJoySalvation1 on Twitter

- YouTube channel: Kingdom Cause Community

We have set up a consultancy company called K3C and we are now helping others who have found themselves addicted or struggling to overcome lust and sex addiction issues. K3C (Kingdom Free Consultancy) is about setting the captives free and taking them from 'bondage to burning' as we believe only a life fully alive in Christ can really break this kind of stronghold.

We post regular videos and teaching for free on our You Tube channel 'K3C' but we recommend booking a personal appointment with us either at our ministry base in Luton or via Skype or FaceTime. This will help us to asses exactly where you are at and what we need to do to ensure you come into the joy of freedom.

You do not (and cannot) do this alone and we would love to walk with you or ensure the right person from our team is.

Please email us at kingdomfreeconsultants@gmail.com and visit our website k3c.co.uk for more details.

We would love to hear from you on how this book has helped you and to see if we can support you further.

Do look out for Rob's follow up book titled *The Joy of Freedom* in 2019. This book is about discovering the joy that freedom from sin and shame brings. It is about learning to greatly value this freedom and how to defend it so you never return to the old way of life. We highly recommend you read this book as it ensures a better balance and authority in keeping the freedom Jesus died to give you. To reserve a copy, please email:

rob.joy@kingdomcause.community